Old Testament Survey

LAW AND HISTORY

BY

SAMUEL J. SCHULTZ, TH.D.

Professor of Bible and Theology

Wheaton College, Wheaton, Illinois

EVANGELICAL TEACHER TRAINING ASSOCIATION

110 Bridge Street • Box 327

Wheaton, Illinois 60187

Preface

A fascinating experience for all who desire to more clearly understand the workings of God is the study of the Old Testament. Well-known Bible stories take on new dimension as seen in the perspective of a sweeping panoramic overview. A capable teacher of others must first experience spiritual depth and develop in Biblical knowledge. This book of Bible Survey will assist in attaining both these goals.

Dr. Schultz is a recognized Bible scholar who communicates the Old Testament message with a refreshing twentieth-century approach. Scholarship is retained within the framework of a challengingly spiritual approach. His comprehensive work on the Old Testament, *The Old Testament Speaks*, is an excellent source of more detailed consideration of this same portion of the Word.

No text, however, can ever substitute for a study of the Bible itself. Nor can the most capable of men apply the message of the Book to the hearts of men. The one who would benefit most from this study must first read the portion of the Word of God under consideration. Read it as many times as possible. Read it in various good translations. Read it; then read it again.

Each chapter of the textbook is followed by suggested questions and exploration activities. Questions are content centered and can profitably be used for reviewing historical fact and development. The project and discussion portion will direct thinking to deeper study of the Word and to consideration of practical application of its message.

Since "the New is in the Old concealed and the Old is in the New revealed," a study of the Old Testament is imperative foundation for clarity of both Old and New Testament Bible teaching. It will enrich a believer's knowledge and life, and make for better teaching to the glory of God. This text and course is highly recommended.

PAUL E. LOTH, Ed.D., *President*
Evangelical Teacher Training Association

SECOND EDITION
Sixth Printing 1979

Library of Congress catalog card number: 64-10037
ISBN: 0-910566-01-1

Printed in U.S.A.

Table of Contents

Charts

Maps

Old Testament Chronology

DATES	BIBLE EVENTS	CONTEMPORARY CULTURES
Period of Beginnings	Genesis 1—11	Prehistorical era
Ca. 2000 B.C. to Ca. 1800 B.C.	The Patriarchs Abraham Isaac Jacob Joseph	Patriarchal narratives reflect culture of Mesopotamia and Egypt
to		
Ca. 1400 B.C.	Israelites reside in Egypt	Egypt enslaves Israelites
to Ca. 1100 B.C.	Moses Joshua The Judges	Palestine occupied Various nations oppress Israel
to Ca. 931 B.C.	Samuel Saul David Solomon The Divided Kingdom	Surrounding nations defeated by Israel
	South *North* Rehoboam Jeroboam I	Syrian Kingdom 931-732
Ca. 875 B.C.	Jehoshaphat Ahab	
Ca. 790 B.C.	Uzziah Jeroboam II	
732 B.C.		Fall of Syria
722 B.C.	Fall of Samaria	
716 B.C.	Hezekiah	Assyrian domination of Palestine 745-650
640 B.C.	Josiah	
586 B.C.	Fall of Jerusalem	Babylonian supremacy 625-539
539 B.C.	Return of the Jews	Medo-Persian rule 539-331
520-515 B.C.	Second Temple Haggai Zechariah	
457 B.C.	Ezra	
444 B.C.	Nehemiah Malachi	

Ca. is a contraction of "circa" meaning "approximately."

CHAPTER ONE

Beginnings

The Bible is the world's best seller. The message of God is considered so vital to man that translators and Bible agencies have produced parts of the Scriptures in more than 1,200 languages. At least 95% of the world's population has portions of the Scriptures in a language available to them.

WHY STUDY THE OLD TESTAMENT The Old Testament has had the widest acclaim of all writings in the fields of literature, history, and religion. Jews, Muslims, and Christians find their beginnings in the Old Testament. It continues to attract and challenge the keenest scholars and meet the needs of even the humblest of every generation.

In contemporary Christianity, the Old Testament is more neglected than the New. Because of the prominence of law in the Old Testament, and of the Gospel in the New, readers do not always clearly understand that God's grace operated throughout the history of His dealings with men. Those who portray the God of the Old Testament as a God of wrath and judgment, and think of God in the New Testament as a God of love, should not ignore the fact that Moses (Deut. 4—6), Jeremiah (9:23, 24), and others represented Him as the God of love and justice. The Apostle Paul, who was thoroughly versed in the Old Testament, called God the "Father of mercies" (II Cor. 1:3).

The Old Testament provides the historical background by which we are able to understand the New. This is apparent in the fact that the New Testament contains over 600 references or allusions to the Old. Jesus and the apostles constantly appealed to it in their teaching. Paul used the Old Testament with great effectiveness as he went from synagogue to synagogue to convince the Jews that Jesus was the Christ (cf. Acts 17:3, 11-13; 18:5, and others). Neither human nature nor God has changed since Old Testament times. Our study of man's relationship with God guides us today and leads us to the proper response of faith and obedience.

THE HISTORY OF OLD TESTAMENT TIMES The history of the Old Testament is found primarily in the first seventeen books (Gen.-Esther) of our English Bible. After a brief account of the developments from Adam to Terah, biblical history is basically concerned with God's chosen nation beginning with Abraham (ca. 2000 B.C.), and continuing until the time of the rebuilding of the walls of Jerusalem under Nehemiah (ca. 450 B.C.). The poetic and prophetic books reflect various periods of history and allow insight into prevailing political, religious, and cultural situations.

As we may learn from the Old Testament itself, the historical books are more than the national records of the Jewish nation, and tell us more than its history. Both Jews and Christians hold that the Old Testament discloses God's revelation of Himself to man. Jesus gave it His stamp of approval as Holy Writ and taught that it had predicted His coming (Luke 24:44, and others). Paul called Old Testament Scripture the oracles of God (Rom. 3:2).

While it is sacred history, the Old Testament gives an account of natural events, guided by and interwoven with the supernatural activity of God. In times of both blessing and adversity in Israel, God was accomplishing His purposes in national and international developments. Consequently, the Old Testament can be interpreted properly, only when both the natural and the supernatural are recognized in its pages.

Old Testament history may be conveniently divided into the following periods:

I. The Era of Beginnings	Genesis 1—11
II. Patriarchal Times	Genesis 12—50
III. Israel Becomes a Nation	Exodus — Deuteronomy
IV. Conquest and Occupation	Joshua, Judges, Ruth
V. The United Kingdom	I Samuel; II Samuel; I Chronicles; II Chronicles 1—9; I Kings 1—11
VI. The Divided Kingdom	I Kings 12—II Kings 25; II Chronicles 10—36
VII. The Post-Exilic Era	Ezra, Esther, Nehemiah

ERA OF BEGINNINGS SCRIPTURE SURVEY: Genesis 1—11

EXTENT OF TIME: From the beginning to about 2000 B.C. Genesis 1—11 is introductory to the whole Bible. In spite of its brevity, this section covers a longer span of time than the rest of the Old Testament; that is, from Abraham to Malachi. Throughout the Scriptures, there are numerous references which amplify and expound the meaning of this brief section. These chapters are essential to a proper understanding of the whole written revelation.

This introduction is vital to the rest of Genesis and to the other four books of the Pentateuch. Beginning with Genesis 12, God's promise of redemption is focused on Abraham and his family. Exodus through Deuteronomy describes an established nation under Moses' leadership, growing out of the descendants of the patriarchs. Moses, who was intimately associated with the events and laws recorded in these four books, is recognized throughout the Bible as the author of the five books called the Pentateuch. Both written and oral sources available to Moses may have provided him with the basic material for Israel's history as recorded in Genesis. Consequently, the book of Genesis is properly regarded as Moses' introduction to the rest of the Pentateuch (cf. Gen. 17:12; John 7:23).

The period of beginnings may be outlined as follows:

I. The Account of Creation   Genesis 1:1—2:25
    A. The universe and its contents, 1:1—2:4a
    B. Man in his first dwelling place, 2:4b-25
II. The Fall of Man and Its Consequences   3:1—6:10
    A. Man's disobedience and expulsion, 3:1-24
    B. Cain and Abel, 4:1-24
    C. The generation of Adam, 4:25—6:10
III. The Flood: God's judgment on Man   6:11—8:19
    A. Preparation for the flood, 6:11-22
    B. The deluge, 7:1—8:19
IV. Man's New Beginning   8:20—11:32
    A. The covenant with Noah, 8:20—9:19
    B. Noah and his sons, 9:20—10:32
    C. The Tower of Babel, 11:1-9
    D. Shem and his descendants, 11:10-32

THE CREATION ACCOUNT   SCRIPTURE SURVEY: Genesis 1—2

Simple but profound is this account of the origin of the universe, and in particular of God's creative activity as manifested on the earth. The record assumes the existence of God who created the universe including the earth and all life upon it. The account clearly states that God created all things. God is the subject of the verb, here as well as in most places where this verb appears. Whenever an object is used with this verb, no pre-existing material is indicated. Although *bara* normally refers to creation *ex nihilo* (out of nothing), it sometimes expresses God's creative power in history (Ex. 34:10; Num. 16:30; Jer. 31:22; Isa. 45:7, 8; 48:7).

A. A divine plan in creation

Order and purpose are expressly stated. Genesis 1:2b is widely interpreted to refer to a divine restoration of a chaotic condition. In this view, the opening verse (1:1) presents an original creation that was subsequently reduced to chaos (1:2a) through judgment and destruction. Usually Isaiah 45:18 is quoted in favor of this view, interpreting the Hebrew word *bohu* to mean "void." Further support is adduced by equating the "prince of Tyre" in Ezekiel 28 with Satan himself and applying Jeremiah 4:23-26 to a pre-Adamic condition. According to this view, verses 1 and 2 represent the summary of all that the Scriptures reveal of God's original creation, and the following verses are an account of the process of restoration. This is known as the Gap-Restoration view.

On the other hand, it is reasonable to interpret this account of creation as giving an orderly series of divine acts in which verse 2 is simply one logical step in the process of creation. Taking this view of the passage, we may see an orderly preparation being made for proper conditions to maintain life on earth, as follows:

1. Heaven and earth were created to provide the basis for an orderly state.
2. Atmospheric conditions were regulated.
3. Dry land was established above the receding water level to make vegetation possible.
4. Lights or luminaries which very likely were included in creation (1:1) were made available to regulate time and the cycles of rotation and revolution of the earth and moon.
5. Animal life appeared on the earth.
6. Man representing the epitome of God's creative acts was placed on the earth as a responsible individual.

On the whole, modern geology presents the same order as given in the Scriptures.

The amount of time required for this process is not indicated in the account, beyond the statements that the whole period of creation is summarized by or in some sense related to six days. The length of each day is not stated, and consequently many varied interpretations have been offered. In the first eleven chapters, not to mention the rest of the Bible, the word "day" may refer to a long period of time (2:4) or to a 24-hour period (8:12). Those holding to the 24-hour day interpretation, usually accept the Gap-Restoration theory of 1:2b.

B. God as Creator and Sustainer

Throughout the first unit of this account of creation the name of "God" (Elohim) is used, whereas beginning at chapter 2:4b the composite name "Lord God" (or "Jehovah God" in the ASV) occurs. The former word portrays God in His relationship to the universe and all contained therein as the great Creator (cf. Col. 1:16; Heb. 1:2). The latter term speaks of God in His relationship to mankind as the One who lovingly cares and provides for him. While man appears only toward the end of the account in Genesis 1, it is immediately clear that he is the center of interest beginning with chapter 2:4b.

C. Man's relationship to creation

The biblical view of man is that of a highly intelligent and responsible being. Clearly distinct from and superior to animals when God created him, Adam was given the privilege of naming the animals, ruling over them, and tilling the Garden of Eden. He was capable of fellowship with God.

The distinction between man and animals is further apparent in the fact that man found no companionship until God created Eve to be his mate (i.e., "a helpmeet for him," 2:20). God's loving care for mankind may be clearly seen in the provision of the Garden of Eden for man's enjoyment and occupation.

MAN'S FALL AND SCRIPTURE SURVEY: Genesis 3:1—6:10
ITS CONSEQUENCES Man's fall into sin is the most significant event in his personal history prior to the coming of Christ to provide redemption for him. We are dependent upon God's revelation concerning the origin of man and his fall, since the fall took place before any written records. Various Scriptures assert that the history of man's fall and its consequences is literal, especially I Timothy 2:13, 14.

A. Adam and Eve's disobedience and expulsion

The crucial issue in Adam and Eve's relationship with God was their disobedience. They yielded to the tempter and were disobedient because of doubt and defiance. It is clear from passages such as John 8:44, Romans 16:20, II Corinthians 11:3, Revelation 12:9 and 20:2, that the serpent stood for more than the physical presence of the reptile. Judgment was solemnly pronounced on all parties—the serpent and Satan, Eve and Adam. However, mercy preceded judgment—a principle that is seen frequently in Scripture—in the Messianic promise that the seed of the woman would be victorious over the seed of the serpent (3:15). Messianic promises were later amplified in Genesis 12:1-3; Numbers 24:17, 19; I Chronicles 17:11-14; Isaiah 7:14; 9:6, 7, and others. The promise of a Savior was given to them in the Garden of Eden, before they were expelled and subjected to the effects of the curse. God's gracious provision of skins as a covering is a hint of the shedding of blood as the means of redemption.

B. Man's hope of redemption

The hope of redemption from the punishment meted out to Adam and Eve is expressed by Eve when Cain is born (4:1). After they were disappointed in Cain, and over the death of Abel, Adam and Eve renewed their expectation upon the birth of Seth (4:25). Later generations cherished the hope of obtaining relief from the curse, as in the case of Lamech, who prophesied at the birth of Noah (5:28-30). And from generation to generation, the promise of redemption through the seed of the woman was passed along.

C. The first murder

Cain became the first murderer. His willful defiance was evident when he brought a sacrifice that did not please God. It seems reasonable to infer from subsequent developments that God had made known what kind of sacrifice was required, and that Cain acted contrary to those instructions. When Abel's sacrifice was accepted by the Lord, Cain was provoked to murder his brother.

D. The ungodly line of Cain

The civilization of Cain and his descendants is summarized in a genealogy which may cover an extended period of time (Gen. 4:17-24). We read that Cain built a city. Its inhabitants were largely dedicated to raising flocks and herds. In the course of time arts developed, and musical instruments were invented. The science of metallurgy came with the extensive use of bronze and iron. It seems, then, that the people began to have a false sense of security. Lamech, the first polygamist, displayed an attitude of scoffing and boasting, priding himself that he could destroy life with his superior weapons. Any recognition of or reference to God is conspicuously absent from the record of Cain's descendants.

E. The godly line of Seth

After the murder of Abel, and with the birth of Seth (4:25 ff.), Adam and Eve's hope was renewed. In the days of Enos men began to turn to God. Generations and centuries later another godly man appeared in the person of Enoch. His life of fellowship with God did not end with death but with his translation. And when Noah was born, as noted above, his father Lamech expressed again the hope that mankind would be relieved of the curse under which it had suffered since Adam and Eve were expelled from Eden.

————

THE FLOOD: SCRIPTURE SURVEY: Genesis 6:11—8:19
GOD'S JUDGMENT   In the days of Noah, godlessness reached a new intensity that brought about judgment from God. Man increasingly used God's good gifts for his own pleasure, and ignored the Giver. Corruption and violence increased so that all man's doings were full of evil. God is said to have regretted the creation of man, and planned to destroy the race from off the earth (6:17). Again mercy preceded judgment in that man was warned of impending destruction over a period of one hundred and twenty years. While the race as a whole continued to corrupt the earth and increase in its lust for power, God assured Noah that He would establish His covenant with him and his descendants (6:12, 18).

God commanded Noah to build an ark that would provide safety for them during the coming flood. This ark, which was 450-600 feet long, 75-100 feet wide, and 45-60 feet deep (depending on the exact length of the cubit) provided enough room for two of each of the unclean species, and for seven each of the clean. For just over one year life was preserved in the ark according to God's provision and instruction.

The deluge was the most universal and severe judgment upon the human race in Old Testament times. Its purpose was to destroy sinful humanity and at the same time renew the human race through a godly remnant. Only Noah and his family escaped death. Subsequent references to this divine judgment point to it as a warning for the rest of mankind (cf. Luke 17: 27; Heb. 11:7; I Pet. 3:20; II Pet. 2:5, 3:3-7). Through the flood God's purpose was accomplished and His covenant established, this time with Noah and his family.

MAN'S NEW BEGINNINGS SCRIPTURE SURVEY: Genesis 8:20—11:32
Man found a new opportunity in a renovated world. Noah's first act after leaving the ark was to worship God with an animal sacrifice.

A. God's covenant with Noah

The rainbow was a sign of the covenant between God and man, assuring him that the human race would never again be destroyed by a flood. Noah and his sons, after receiving the basis for a new hope, were commissioned to repopulate and possess the earth. God now provided for their sustenance, giving them animals, properly slaughtered, and plant life for food. All men, however, would be held strictly accountable to God for shedding the blood of other men.

Canaan, a son of Ham, was cursed because of Ham's disrespectful treatment of Noah. Many centuries later the Canaanites were divinely judged when the Israelites, under Joshua, were commanded to destroy them.

B. The Tower of Babel

While it was a racial and linguistic unit, the human race remained for an indefinite period in one area (11:1-9). In defiance of God's command to spread abroad over the earth, and out of pride in their own achievements, they undertook to build the Tower of Babel on the Plain of Shinar. But God intervened and put an end to their endeavor by confusing their language. Consequently the race was scattered according to God's original intention.

C. The dispersion of Noah's sons

The geographic and ethnic distribution of the human race is described in chapter 10. Japheth and his sons moved westward toward Spain via the Caspian and Black Seas (10:2-5). The sons of Ham migrated southwestward to Africa (10:6-14), while the Semites (10:21-31) occupied the area north of the Persian Gulf.

D. The Messianic line of Shem

The record of the developments during the age of beginnings is finally narrowed down to the Semites (11:1-32). By means of a genealogical listing of ten generations, the record focuses attention upon Terah, who migrated from Ur to Haran. A climax is reached upon the introduction of Abram, whose name is later changed to Abraham (17:5). He became the father and founder of a chosen nation, Israel. Within that nation were the hopes of universal blessing, and for the fulfillment of the Messianic promises (Gen. 22:15-18; cf. Matt. 1:1, 2). The rest of the Old Testament is principally the history and literature of God's chosen people, Israel.

Guide Questions for Study and Discussion

1. Why is the study of the Old Testament basic to understanding the New Testament?
2. List the historical divisions of the Old Testament era.
3. Outline briefly the period of beginnings.
4. List the events for the days of creation in order.
5. What responsibilities were assigned to Adam and Eve?
6. What was the crucial issue in Adam and Eve's relationship with God?
7. How was God's mercy manifested in the account of the fall?
8. What were the moral causes of the flood?
9. What was the sign and significance of the covenant with Noah?
10. What motivated the descendants of Noah to build the Tower of Babel?

Activities for Enrichment and Application

1. Trace the steps of disobedience in the story of the fall of man. Compare and contrast this with man's behavior today.
2. Write a paragraph to explain the emphasis the New Testament puts upon the following events:
   Creation (cf. John 1:1, 2; Acts 14:15; Heb. 1:10; 11:3; Rev. 4:11; 10:6)
   Man created in the image of God (I Cor. 11:7; Col. 3:10; James 3:9)
   The Flood (Matt. 24:37-39; Luke 17:26, 27; I Pet. 3:20)
3. Compare and contrast the line of Seth with the line of Cain. Relate this to the spiritual man and the natural man.
4. Trace the evidence of God's interest in man in Genesis 1—11. Give at least five evidences of His interest in mankind today.

Significant Resources

DAVIS, JOHN D. "Chronology" in Davis Dictionary of the Bible. Grand Rapids: Baker Book House, 1954.

MORRIS, HENRY M., & WHITCOMB, JOHN C., JR. The Genesis Flood. Philadelphia: Presbyterian & Reformed Pub. Co., 1961.

RAMM, BERNARD. The Christian View of Science and Scripture. Grand Rapids: Wm. B. Eerdmans Pub. Co., 1955.

SCHULTZ, SAMUEL J. The Old Testament Speaks. New York: Harper & Row, 1970.

THOMAS, W. H. GRIFFITH. Genesis: A Devotional Commentary. Grand Rapids: Wm. B. Eerdmans Pub. Co., 1946.

CHAPTER TWO

The Patriarchs

SCRIPTURE SURVEY: Genesis 12—50
EXTENT OF TIME: ca. 2000-1600 B.C.

During the early part of the second millenium B.C., the patriarchs lived in the midst of Near Eastern cultures. Abraham emigrated from the Tigris-Euphrates Valley to Palestine, and Jacob and his sons settled in Egypt at the close of the patriarchal era. The area between the Nile and the Tigris-Euphrates is known as the Fertile Crescent.

At that time the great pyramids had already been constructed in Egypt. In Mesopotamia various codes of law regulating commerce and social relationships had already been written. Merchants traveling with camel and donkey caravans frequently passed through Palestine to carry on trade between the two great cultural centers of the ancient world.

The patriarchal period is covered in Genesis 12—50. It may be outlined as follows:

I. Abraham	Genesis 12:1—25:18
II. Isaac and Jacob	25:19—36:43
III. Joseph	37:1—50:26

ABRAHAM   Abraham is one of the greatest and best-known characters in history. In both Judaism and Islam, Abraham is a patriarch. In Christianity, he is remembered as a man of great faith, and as the father of the faithful. The chapters dealing with Abraham will be outlined in this way:

I. Abraham Established in Canaan	Genesis 12—14
A. His moves from Haran to Shechem, Bethel, and the South Country, 12:1-9	
B. Sojourn in Egypt, 12:10-20	
C. Separation of Abraham and Lot, 13:1-13	
D. The land promised, 13:14-18	
E. Lot rescued, 14:1-16	
F. Abraham blessed by Melchizedek, 14:17-24	
II. Abraham Awaits the Son Promised To Him	15—24
A. The promise of a son, 15:1-21	
B. Hagar bears Ishmael, 16:1-16	
C. The promise renewed—the sign of the covenant, 17:1-27	

OLD TESTAMENT WORLD

IN THE DAYS OF

THE PATRIARCHS

Scale of Miles

0   100   200

A. Background and time

Abraham was born into an idolatrous family and environment (Josh. 24: 2, 3). His father may have participated in the worship of the moon at Ur, and later at Haran. In response to God's call, Abraham left Haran and traveled into Palestine, about 400 miles away.

Abraham's moves may be traced in the Genesis narrative. Most of the places he visited can be identified today. Shechem, some thirty miles north of Jerusalem, was his first stopping place. Later he lived at nearby Bethel. Near Hebron, tourists can still see the oaks of Mamre where Abraham built an altar and had fellowship with God. Other cities where he lived were Gerar in the Philistine country, and Beersheba, to the south. A trip to Egypt is also noted in the Scriptures.

Most of these chapters deal with the twenty-five years of Abraham's life prior to the birth of Isaac (12—20). Chapters 21—25 give us relatively little detail from the seventy-five remaining years of his life.

1. Temporal prosperity

Genesis tells of the great wealth of Abraham. The statement in 12:5, "all their substance that they had gathered, and the souls that they had gotten in Haran," merely suggests the extent of his riches. But the fact that he could muster a force of 318 trained servants to deliver Lot, indicates that he had vast resources (14:14). The ten-camel caravan used by Abraham's servant on his trip to Mesopotamia points to extensive wealth, since one camel represented a larger investment than the average person could afford (24:10). Servants were added to Abraham's household by purchase, gift, and birth (16:1; 17:23, 27; 20:14). Local chieftains recognized Abraham as a prince, and made alliances and concluded treaties with him (14:13; 21:32; 23:6).

2. Customs and culture

Abraham was a man of his times. His decision to sojourn in Egypt when pressured by famine, may indicate a lack of faith; and his behavior before Pharaoh definitely represents a period of spiritual declension. As Sarah's husband, he might have been killed. But as her brother, he expected to be honored. Decency and strict truthfulness were both bypassed, and Abraham was later ushered out of Egypt in disgrace (12:11-20).

Laws prevalent in the Mesopotamian culture from which Abraham came, also explain why he considered making his eldest servant Eliezer his heir (15:1-3). Nuzu laws provided that if a man and his wife were childless, they could adopt a servant as a son with full legal rights, and the assurance of receiving the inheritance in return for constant care and proper burial at death. As Abraham weighed this possibility, God renewed His promise (15:4, 5).

At Sarah's suggestion, Abraham accepted the idea of having a son by Hagar, Sarah's handmaid. This, too, was in agreement with the custom of the age. A childless couple could also adopt the son of a handmaid as a legal heir. After ten years in Canaan, without any prospect of the promised son, Abraham and Sarah may have expected that this method would bring about the fulfillment of God's promise. Thirteen years later, when Abraham was ninety-nine, God rejected these plans and this time assured him that Sarah would bear him the promised son. At this time the covenant was renewed and circumcision was instituted as its visible sign (17:1-27; cf. 12:1-3; 13:14-18; 15:18-21; Col. 2:11).

There was another spiritual lapse in Abraham's life when he lied about his wife to Abimelech at Gerar (20:1-18). However, God intervened on Abraham's behalf so that he was enabled to pray for the king and his household.

From the expulsion of Hagar (21:9-21), and Abraham's concern for her welfare, it appears that he had contemporary laws in mind. It was illegal to sell a handmaid into slavery after she had given birth to a child for her master. While the case is not strictly parallel, Abraham expelled Hagar only after he had God's assurance that this was His will. Even then he made provision for her and her son when they departed.

Again, when Sarah died, Abraham is seen as a man of his times. When he bargained with the Hittites for a burial place (23:1-20), he wanted to purchase only the cave of Machpelah. However, Ephron insisted on selling the field with the cave. In this way, Abraham also became subject to taxation under Hittite law. Had he acquired only the cave, he might have been free from that liability.

B. A man of faith

Through faith in God's promises, Abraham rose above the religious level of his times. From the beginning he responded with obedience. Wherever Abraham sojourned in Canaan, he erected an altar and gave public testimony of the fact that he worshiped "the God of heaven and earth" (24:3) in the midst of a pagan environment (cf. 12:7, 8 ff.).

Consider the sixfold promise God made to Abraham:

1. "I will make of thee a great nation."
2. "I will bless thee."
3. "I will make thy name great."
4. "Thou shalt be a blessing."
5. "I will bless them that bless thee and curse him that curseth thee."
6. "In thee shall all the families of the earth be blessed."

This multiple promise has had far-reaching implications in history down to the present time—more extensive than Abraham could comprehend during his lifetime. It is true that Abraham was richly blessed while he lived, and before his death he could understand that many nations could yet be born through Ishmael, Isaac, and others of his sons. Today, by way of contrast, the name of Abraham is held in great honor among Jews, Muslims, and Christians. The promise that Abraham would be a blessing to all the families of the earth unfolds in Christ. Matthew begins his Gospel with the assertion that Jesus—the Savior of the world—is the "son of Abraham" (1:1; cf. Gal. 3:6-9).

C. The Abrahamic Covenant

As we study the life of Abraham in subsequent chapters, it is apparent that Abraham's grasp of the promises was progressively enlarged. In times of crisis Abraham gained fuller understanding of them. He showed great generosity when he offered Lot the choice of the land (chap. 13). While Lot's decision was based on the prospects of immediate material gain in a godless environment, Abraham received confirmation from God that the land was to be his, and for his posterity.

When Abraham rescued Lot, he refused to accept a reward from the king of Sodom, and was concerned about the legal arrangements for the future. But God revealed to Abraham more about the time to come. He promised that his descendants would be as numerous as the stars of heaven, but that they would dwell in Egypt for 400 years. We read that Abraham believed God, and that it was accounted to him for righteousness (cf. Rom. 4:3, 22).

God's covenant with Abraham was enlarged and confirmed when Abraham was ninety-nine years old. The terms of the covenant were distinctly given (17:1-27). While the birth of the promised son was still a year away, circumcision was given as the distinctive sign of the covenant, for Abraham and his descendants (cf. Rom. 4:9-12).

D. A friend of God

It may be seen from Genesis 18 and 19 that there was friendship between Abraham and God (cf. Isa. 41:8; James 2:22, 23). When God shared with Abraham the secret of His plans concerning Sodom and Gomorrah, Abraham was moved to prayer. He rested his case with the rhetorical question, "Shall not the God of all the earth do right?" God showed that His justice was tempered by mercy when He assured Abraham that the cities would be saved if ten righteous people were found in them. Only because there were not that many the cities were destroyed, though Lot and his family were rescued.

E. More testings and trials

Abraham faced the greatest test of his faith after Isaac's birth. God asked him to sacrifice his only son on Mount Moriah. Abraham obeyed, exhibiting faith that God was able to raise men from the dead (cf. Heb. 11:19). He was obliged to give an answer to the most disturbing question ever posed by a son when Isaac asked about the sacrifice. By faith Abraham reached beyond the visible evidence to give a prophetic reply, assuring Isaac that God Himself would provide the sacrifice (22:1-19; cf. I Cor. 5:7; Heb. 9:26; Rev. 13:8). First God provided a ram, and centuries later, His own beloved Son.

ABRAHAM'S SEED   Isaac was Abraham's son to whom God's promises would be repeated.

The story of the way Abraham provided a bride for Isaac (chap. 24) is fascinating and exciting. The account contains numerous lessons in the way God guided Abraham's servant through prayer. Finally he was able to take Rebekah back to the land of patriarchal promise to be Isaac's wife.

The Scriptures tell us little about him. His life was uneventful in comparison to that of his father and his sons. He lived most of his life in southern Canaan in the vicinity of Gerar, Rehoboth and Beersheba. Isaac was a necessary link in the process of fulfilling God's promises to Abraham. From the record (27:27-33) we recognize him as a man of faith who invoked future blessings upon his sons (cf. Heb. 11:20).

I. The Family of Isaac   Genesis 25:18-34
   A. Rebekah the mother of twins, 25:19-26
   B. Esau and Jacob exchange birthrights, 25:27-34
II. Isaac Established in Canaan   26:1-33
   A. The covenant confirmed to Isaac, 26:1-5
   B. Troubles with Abimelech, 26:6-22
   C. God's blessing in Isaac, 26:23-33
III. The Patriarchal Blessing   26:34—28:9
   A. Isaac favors Esau, 26:34—27:4
   B. Blessing stolen—immediate consequences, 27:5—28:9

Abraham had other sons. The best known of these were Ishmael, the father of the Arabs, and Midian, the father of the Midianites. To each of these other sons Abraham gave gifts as they went out from Canaan, leaving the territory to Isaac, the heir of all of Abraham's possessions.[1]

---

[1]For a more extensive study of Abraham, Isaac, and Jacob, see Charles Pfeiffer, *The Patriarchal Age*, (Grand Rapids: Baker Book House, 1961).

TWIN BROTHERS A study of the lives of Isaac's two sons, Esau and Jacob, is both intriguing and disappointing. Jacob took advantage of Esau in buying the birthright—the right of the first-born to preeminence in the tribe—and connived with his mother Rebekah to deceive Isaac and steal the blessing. On the other hand, Esau lacked faith in God, a true sense of values, and appreciation for his birthright (25:29-34). Later he disregarded the ideals of his parents and married a Hittite woman (26:34). The author of Hebrews calls him "profane" or "irreligious." The history of Esau's descendants, the Edomites, deserves separate study.

A. Jacob's adventures

Although Jacob left Canaan with his father's blessing, he passed through many hard experiences before he became a man of faith. He was afraid that Esau would seek revenge. His parents, hoping to keep him from marrying a Hittite woman, sent him to Mesopotamia. On the way, while he slept at Bethel, Jacob had a dream and responded to God with a tentative commitment. Jacob prospered greatly while he worked for Laban, acquiring not only a large family, but great wealth in flocks.

B. Back to Canaan

Conscious now of God's direction, Jacob made plans to return to Canaan. A strained relationship had developed between Jacob and Laban, and Jacob took the opportunity to depart while Laban was on a sheep-shearing mission. Laban pursued him quickly, but since Jacob had a three-day advantage, he reached the hill-country of Gilead before Laban overtook him. Laban claimed that his household gods had been taken. The teraphim, which Rachel hid beneath her skirts, undoubtedly had more than mere religious significance for Laban. According to Nuzu law, a son-in-law who possessed the household gods might claim the family inheritance in court. Though Laban could not find the idol, he nullified any advantage that might accrue to Jacob by means of a covenant between Jacob and himself, barring Jacob from the land.

At the Jabbok River Jacob learned that Esau was coming against him with 400 men. In order to appease Esau, he sent his possessions and family, with gifts for his brother, ahead of him. Through the night he wrestled with an assailant whom he sensed to be God Himself. In that encounter his name was changed from "Jacob" to "Israel," meaning "he who strives with God." The blessing implied in the new name expressed a new relationship: hereafter, Jacob would not be the deceiver; instead, he would have victory with God.

After being reconciled with his brother, Jacob moved southward to Shechem. There Levi and Simeon aroused the enmity of the community through scandal and treachery (34:1-31). As Jacob separated to move to Bethel, where he had previously made a commitment to God, he removed the remaining idolatry from his household. At Bethel he built an altar, and in response, God renewed His covenant, assuring him that a company of nations and kings should emanate from Israel (35:9-15).

Eventually, Jacob settled in Hebron, the home of his father Isaac. While they were on the way, Rachel died and was buried in the vicinity of Bethlehem. Later, when Isaac died, Esau came from Seir where he had settled, to accompany his brother Jacob at the burial of their father.

THE LIFE OF JOSEPH Joseph, Rachel's older son, was Jacob's pride and joy. Jacob made him a full-length tunic which, according to the Septuagint and the Targum Jonathan, was "a coat of many colors." It seems that such a coat was the distinctive mark of a tribal chief. Joseph's older brothers already hated him because he reported their evil conduct to Jacob. Now they hated him all the more. And when Joseph's dreams indicated that he would be exalted over them, they sold him to Ishmaelite and Midianite traders who were passing by their camp at Dothan. When Joseph was taken into Egypt, his brothers never expected to see him again. They led their father, Jacob, to believe that Joseph had been torn to pieces by wild animals.

I. Joseph the Favorite Son	Genesis 37
A. Hated by his brethren, 37:1-24	
B. Sold to Egypt, 37:25-36	
II. Judah and Tamar[2]	38
III. Joseph—a Slave and a Ruler	39—41
A. Joseph demoted to prison, 39:1-20	
B. Interpreting dreams, 39:21—41:36	
C. Ruler next to Pharaoh, 40:37-57	

---

[2]For a discussion of this chapter, see Samuel J. Schultz, *The Old Testament Speaks*, p. 39.

A. A slave in Egypt

Whether there was adversity and suffering, or success, over the years that Joseph spent in Egypt, he continually honored God. Because he did not want to sin against God, nor against his master, he would not yield to the temptation put before him by Potiphar's wife (39:9). When he was asked to interpret dreams, Joseph gave God the credit for the ability to do so (40:8). He also acknowledged God before Pharaoh, boldly asserting that, through Pharaoh's dream, God was revealing that a specific number of years of plenty and famine were to follow (41:14-36). In naming his son Manasseh (which means "forgetting," 41:51), he testified that God had helped him to forget his sorrow. When he revealed his identity to his brothers, he acknowledged that God had brought him to Egypt. After Jacob's death, Joseph reassured them that God had ordered the events of history for the good of all, and that they should not fear him as though he were in God's place (50:15-21).

B. Savior of his family

Joseph's recognition of God, and his trust in Him through many difficulties, was rewarded by his promotion. In Potiphar's house he was so trustworthy that he was made the overseer. Later, though imprisoned on false charges, he soon became the warden, and was able to use his position to help his fellow prisoners. A butler, who for two years had forgotten Joseph's help, suddenly remembered, and arranged to have Joseph brought before Pharaoh to interpret his dreams. This was an opportune moment— Pharaoh needed the help of a man of wisdom such as Joseph. Now as chief administrator for Pharaoh, Joseph guided Egypt through the crucial years of plenty and famine, and incidentally saved his own family from starvation. His position of power enabled him to allot the broad pasturelands of Goshen to the Israelites when they migrated to Egypt. There they were able to tend their flocks, and those of Pharoah as well.

Jacob's words of blessing provide a fitting conclusion to the patriarchal age. We may regard his deathbed pronouncements as his last will and testament. Though he was in Egypt, his oral blessing would be legal and binding. And in keeping with God's promises, Jacob's blessing was also prophetic.

Before Joseph died in Egypt, he voiced his confidence in the covenant that God had made with Abraham, Isaac, and Jacob. The promises had been faithfully conveyed to each generation, and Joseph believed that God would fulfill them in bringing the Israelites back to the land which had been promised to them (cf. Gen. 15:1-21; 50:24-26).

Guide Questions for Study and Discussion

1. Who were the patriarchs?
2. Outline the main events of Abraham's life.
3. Why were the altars Abraham built to worship God especially significant?
4. Why is Abraham called a man of faith?
5. What was the sign and significance of God's covenant with Abraham?
6. How did Abraham's servant discern God's guidance in choosing Isaac's bride?
7. Describe the circumstances leading to Joseph's release from prison in Egypt.
8. In what ways did Joseph indicate forgiveness toward his brothers when they came to Egypt?

Activities for Enrichment and Application

1. Trace the patriarchal promise in Genesis 12—50. What is its significance today?
2. On a map, locate the cities associated with the patriarchs. Which of these have prophetic significance today?
3. Note the origin of the following peoples in Genesis: Moabites, Ammonites, Midianites, Arabs, and Edomites. Which of these are in world news today?
4. Compare and contrast the characters of Jacob and Esau. What particular personality traits make them typical of mankind?
5. What do the following New Testament references reveal about these Genesis characters?

    Abraham (Rom. 4:1-22; Gal. 3:16, 17; 4:22-31; Heb. 11:17, 18)
    Isaac (Luke 13:28; Rom. 9:7, 10; Gal. 4:28; Heb. 11:9, 18; James 2:21)
    Esau (Rom. 9:13; Heb. 12:16, 17)
    Jacob (Matt. 1:2; 8:11; Luke 13:28; John 4:12; Rom. 9:13; Heb. 11:9, 20, 21)
    Joseph (Acts 7:11-14; Heb. 11:21, 22; Rev. 7:8)
6. What laws and customs seemed to influence the behavior of the patriarchs? To what extent should culture govern Christian ethics? Suggest at least two cultural factors which involve the question of Christian standards. Discuss the practical Biblical solution to these.

Significant Resources

ALBRIGHT, WILLIAM F. *The Archaeology of Palestine*. Glouster, MA: Peter Smith Publisher, 1960.

FINEGAN, JACK. *Light from the Ancient Past. The Archaeological Background of Judaism and Christianity*. 2nd ed. Princeton, NJ: Princeton Univ. Press, 1959.

FREE, JOSEPH P. *Archaeology and Bible History*. 5th ed. rev. Wheaton, IL: Scripture Press, 1976.

PFEIFFER, CHARLES F. *The Book of Genesis*. Grand Rapids: Baker Book House, 1958.

UNGER, MERRILL F. *Archaeology and the Old Testament*. Grand Rapids: Zondervan Pub. House, 1954.

WISEMAN, D. J. "The Patriarchal Age" in *The New Bible Dictionary*. Ed. by J. D. Douglas. Grand Rapids: Wm. B. Eerdmans Pub. Co., 1962.

CHAPTER THREE

God's Holy Nation

SCRIPTURE SURVEY: Exodus—Leviticus
EXTENT OF TIME: ca. 1600-1400 B.C.
Sacred history takes on new dimensions with the book of Exodus. Centuries had passed in silence since the death of Joseph. Meanwhile the patriarchal descendants had become exceedingly numerous. A Pharaoh came into power who viewed this growing population with disfavor, enslaving and oppressing them. Under the leadership of Moses the Israelites were delivered from slavery, transformed into an independent nation, and prepared for the conquest and occupation of Canaan.

The spiritual significance of this deliverance can hardly be overemphasized. The rest of the Pentateuch or approximately one-sixth of the entire Old Testament is devoted to this eventful development.

Let us look at the scope of movement and time involved as we preview these four books in the following outline:

I. Israel's Enslavement, 400 years	Exodus 1, 2
II. Egypt to Sinai, less than 1 year	Exodus 3—18
III. Encampment at Sinai, ca. 1 year	Exodus 19—Numbers 10
IV. Wilderness Wanderings, ca. 38 years	Numbers 10—21
V. Encampment Before Canaan, ca. 1 year	Numbers 22—Deuteronomy 34

Egypt was one of the most advanced centers of civilization during the period when Israel emerged as a nation. The New Kingdom began in the sixteenth century with the expulsion of the Hyksos people who had occupied Egypt for nearly two centuries. From about 1550-1100 B.C. Egypt maintained a well-established empire. One of its greatest military leaders was Thutmose III (ca. 1500-1450) who repeatedly marched his armies through Palestine or sailed the Mediterranean to extend Egyptian control to the Euphrates River. He is often compared to Alexander the Great or Napoleon.

FROM SLAVERY In a relatively short period under the leadership of
TO NATIONHOOD Moses, the Israelites were delivered from oppression to an independent nation consciously aware of its covenant relationship with God. The biblical account may be divided as follows:

I. Israel Freed from Slavery   Exodus 1:1—13:19
   A. Conditions in Egypt, 1:1-22
   B. Moses—birth, education, and call, 2:1—4:31
   C. The contest with Pharaoh, 5:1—11:10
   D. The Passover, 12:1—13:19
II. From Egypt to Mount Sinai   13:20—19:2
   A. Divine deliverance, 13:20—15:21
   B. En route to the Sinaitic encampment, 15:22—19:2

A. Oppression of the Israelites

When the clan of Jacob migrated to Egypt, they were favored by the Egyptian rulers who were indebted to Joseph for guiding them successfully through an extensive famine. Settled in the rich fertile grazing area of the land of Goshen in the Nile Delta, the Israelites prospered and increased greatly during a period of several centuries. With the rise of the eighteenth dynasty at the beginning of the New Kingdom, new policies were introduced, designed to alleviate the Pharaoh's fear of a rebellion by the Israelites. Subjected to hard labor assignments in building the cities of Pithom and Rameses (Ex. 1:11), the Israelites multiplied so prolifically that the fears of the Egyptian rulers increased. Not only was the oppression intensified, but an edict was also issued to drown at birth all the male children born to the Israelites (Ex. 1:15-22). Decades later when Moses challenged the power of Pharaoh, the Egyptians even withheld straw (Ex. 5:5-19) which was helpful to the Israelites in producing bricks.

B. Leadership prepared

Dark were the days of Israel's history when Moses was born. Moses, however, was adopted by Pharaoh's daughter, exposed to educational opportunities in the foremost center of civilization, and trained in the wisdom of the Egyptians (Acts 7:22).

The second phase of Moses' training was provided in the desert of Midian where he spent the next forty years. His attempt to help his people ended in failure. In Midian he married Zipporah the daughter of Reuel, a priest of Midian, who was also known as Jethro. While shepherding flocks in the area surrounding the Gulf of Aqaba, Moses acquired a thorough knowledge of this territory even though he was not aware that he would some day lead the nation of Israel through this desert.

Consider the call of Moses (Ex. 3:1—4:17) in the light of his background and knowledge of the royal court in Egypt and the apparently hopeless condition of the Israelites. Moses knew that the Pharaoh of Egypt was not disposed to take orders from anyone. Note the problems Moses realistically reflected and the answers God gave as expressed paraphrastically below:

Moses: "Who am I to face mighty Pharaoh?"
God: "I will be with thee."

Moses: "By whose authority shall I go to face my own people?"
God: "I AM—the God of Abraham, Isaac, and Jacob—sends you."
Moses: "The Israelites will not believe me."
God: "Use the rod in your hand to perform miracles before them."
Moses: "I am not an orator."
God: "I will send Aaron to speak for you."
With this assurance Moses returned to Egypt to do God's bidding.

C. The contest

In a series of ten plagues Moses challenged the might of the Pharaoh of Egypt who persistently refused to release Israel. The purpose of the plagues (Ex. 9:16) was to demonstrate God's mighty power to the Israelites as well as to the Egyptians. Pharaoh had the opportunity of complying with God's will but in the course of this experience, he hardened his heart.[1] His basic attitude never changed. Although the plagues came through natural phenomena, the supernatural power of God was apparent in intensification, in discrimination, and in time control. These plagues may have been directed against the various gods of the Egyptians.

D. The Passover

The Passover and death of the firstborn brought this contest to an eventful climax. Every home in the land was affected. The Egyptian homes were made conscious of the judgment of the God of Israel in the death of the oldest son in each family. The Israelites in every home by contrast were made conscious of God's redeeming power as they put blood on the doorposts, ate the lamb, and then in haste made their journey out of Egypt (cf. Matt. 26:26-28; I Cor. 5:7; Heb. 9:14, 15).

E. The miracle of deliverance

The shortest route from Egypt to Canaan was a well-traveled road along the Mediterranean coast. But Moses, divinely instructed, led this multitude of liberated slaves through the Red Sea to the Sinai Peninsula. The miracle of deliverance was followed by numerous divine interventions and provisions for Israel's safety and sustenance. God's pillar of cloud by day and of fire by night not only served to protect in time of danger, but also to provide guidance en route (cf. I Cor. 10:1).

LAWS FOR A HOLY NATION Israel's religion was a revealed religion. It was not adopted from surrounding nations but stood in sharp

---

[1] Three Hebrew words are used adverting to Pharaoh's attitude, denoting an intensification of a condition already existing. Cf. Joseph P. Free, *Archaeology and Bible History* (Wheaton, IL: Scripture Press, 1976); pp. 93, 94.

contrast to the religious standards and practices of the heathen nations of that period.

The biblical content of God's revelation to Israel at Mount Sinai may be outlined as follows:

I. God's Covenant with Israel   Exodus 19:3—24:8
   A. Preparation for meeting God, 19:3-25
   B. The Decalogue, 20:1-17
   C. Ordinances for Israel, 20:18—23:33
   D. Ratification of the covenant, 24:1-8
II. The Place of Worship   24:9—40:38
   A. Preparation for construction, 24:10—31:18
   B. Idolatry and judgment, 32:1—34:35
   C. Building of the tabernacle, 35:1—40:38
III. Instructions for Holy Living   Leviticus 1:1—27:34
   A. The offerings, 1:1—7:38
   B. The priesthood, 8:1—10:20
   C. Laws of purification, 11:1—15:33
   D. The Day of Atonement, 16:1-34
   E. Heathen customs forbidden, 17:1—18:30
   F. Laws of holiness, 19:1—22:33
   G. Feasts and seasons, 23:1—25:55
   H. Conditions for God's blessings, 26:1—27:34

THE MOSAIC COVENANT Redemption from Egypt obligated Israel to be God's holy nation. God, who had made a covenant with Abraham and his descendants, had delivered the Israelites and entered into a covenant with them as a nation (Ex. 19:3—24:8). The key to a right relationship with God was obedience. Their observance of the laws would result in their being a holy peculiar people and distinguish them from the heathen nations about them.

Most important for the Israelites were the Ten Commandments commonly known as the Decalogue (Ex. 20:1-17). These are usually classified as moral laws and repeated in the New Testament, with the exception of the Sabbath observance. The distinctive feature of the Decalogue sets forth monotheism (worship of one true God), not even allowing the Israelites images. This set Israel apart in sharp contrast to the pagan practices of surrounding nations.

Expansion of these moral laws and additional regulations were designed to guide the Israelites in their conduct (Ex. 21—24; Lev. 11—26). Simple obedience to these moral, civil, and ceremonial laws would mark them as God's holy people. Many of the practices forbidden to Israel were common in Egypt and Canaan. Marriage of brother and sister, practiced in Egypt, was forbidden to the Israelites. Regulations regarding motherhood and childbirth not only reminded the Israelites that man is a sinful creature, but stood in sharp contrast to sex perversion, prostitution, and child sacrifice associated with the religious rites and ceremonies of the Canaanites. In Egypt, the slaughter of animals was associated with idolatry. Some of the restriction in food and slaughter of animals can be better understood in the light of prevailing practices known to the Israelites. It was fitting that the Israelites, having vivid memories of slavery, should be instructed to leave gleanings for the poor at harvest time, provide for the helpless, honor the aged, and constantly render righteous judgment in all their relationships. Many of these civil and ceremonial laws were temporary in nature and were abrogated in the course of time as conditions changed.

THE TABERNACLE In contrast to many temples in Egypt, Israel was to have one sanctuary. Construction of the tabernacle was under the supervision of two foremen, Bezalel and Aholiab, of whom it is stated that they were filled with the "Spirit of God" and "ability and intelligence" to supervise (Ex. 31, 35, 36). Laymen who were motivated to help assisted with building, and freewill offerings were accepted from the people to supply the materials.

The tabernacle itself was 45 feet long and 15 feet wide, divided into two parts. The entrance from the east opened into the holy place 30 feet in length. Beyond it was the Holy of Holies. Surrounding the tabernacle was a court having a perimeter of 450 feet and a 30-foot entrance from the east. The eastern half of this enclosure was the worshiper's square where stood the altar of sacrifice or brazen altar where the Israelites made their sacrifices. Between this altar and the tabernacle was the bronze laver where the priests washed their feet, in preparation for officiating at the altar of sacrifice in the tabernacle.

Three pieces of furniture were in the holy place: on the right was the table of shewbread for the priests, on the left was the golden candlestick, and before the veil separating the holy place from the Holy of Holies was the altar of incense.

The ark of the covenant was the most sacred object in Israel. This and this alone was placed in the Holy of Holies. On the lid of the ark facing each other were two cherubim of gold with their wings overshadowing the place between them known as the mercy seat. This mercy seat represented the presence of God, and unlike the heathen, the Israelites had no material object to represent their God. The *Shekinah* (Hebrew— to dwell) glory of Jehovah God dwelled with Israel in the tabernacle. Here the high priest sprinkled blood once a year on the Day of Atonement in behalf of the nation. Subsequently, there were stored in the ark the Decalogue (Ex. 25:21; 31:18; Deut. 10:3-5), a pot of manna (Ex. 16:34), and Aaron's rod that blossomed (Num. 17:10). Before Israel entered Canaan, the book of the Law was placed next to the ark (Deut. 31:26).

THE PRIESTHOOD   In patriarchal times the head of the family officiated in making a sacrifice. Since the seed of Abraham had become a large nation, it was necessary to have priests officiate for orderly ministration and effective worship. Aaron the brother of Moses was appointed as the high priest, assisted by his sons, two of whom were smitten in judgment for bringing unholy fire into the tabernacle (Num. 3:2-4; Lev. 10:1, 2). By virtue of having escaped death in Egypt, the firstborn of every family belonged to God. Chosen as substitutes for the oldest son in each family, the Levites assisted the priests in their ministration (Num. 3:5-14; 8:17). In this way the entire nation was represented in the priestly ministry.

The priests represented the people before God, officiated in the prescribed offerings (Ex. 28; Lev. 16), taught the Law to the laity, and were responsible for ministering at the tabernacle. The sanctity of the priests as described in Leviticus 21:1—22:10 reflects a contrast with heathen practice.[2]

THE OFFERINGS   The practice of offering sacrifices characterized God-fearing men from the time of man's expulsion from the Garden of Eden. Whether or not the various kinds of offerings were clearly distinguished and known to the Israelites when they left Egypt may be debatable. As a free nation and God's covenant people, they were given specific instructions regarding their sacrifices (Lev. 1—7).

Four kinds of offerings involved the shedding of blood:

1. *Burnt offering*—the distinctive feature was that the entire sacrifice was consumed, signifying complete consecration (cf. Heb. 10:1-3, 10, 11).
2. *Peace offering*—a voluntary offering in which part of the sacrificial animal was eaten by the priest and the offerer, signifying fellowship between God and man (cf. Eph. 2:13, 14).
3. *Sin offering*—this sacrifice was required for sins of ignorance committed inadvertently (cf. John 1:29; 6:51).
4. *Trespass offering*—infringement on the rights of others necessitated this offering and restitution where possible (cf. Col. 2:13).

The grain offering did not involve the shedding of blood but consisted of the products of the soil representing the fruits of man's labor (Lev. 2:1-16; 6:14-23; cf. Mark 8:15; I Cor. 5:8; Gal. 5:9). Apparently this was never brought as an offering by itself but was brought in addition to other offerings. When expiation for sin had been made through the shedding of blood, then the offering of gifts was acceptable to God.

---

[2] For a fuller description of the religion of Israel in its contrast to contemporary heathen practice, see Schultz, *The Old Testament Speaks*, pp. 57-74.

FEASTS AND SEASONS Through appointed feasts and seasons Israelites were constantly reminded that they were
God's holy people. To observe these holy periods was part of their
covenant commitment. Briefly note the times designated for their observance:

1. *Sabbath*—weekly, by rest and cessation from work, they were reminded of God's creative work and their deliverance from Egyptian
   bondage. Note that this was included in the Decalogue (Deut. 5:
   12-15; cf. Mark 2:27, 28).
2. *New Moon and Feast of Trumpets*—trumpet blasts proclaimed the
   beginning of each month. The first day of the seventh month was
   designated as the Feast of Trumpets, ushering in the climax of
   religious observances (Num. 29:1-6; cf. Col. 2:16).
3. *Sabbatical year*—upon entrance into Canaan the Israelites were
   to leave the fields unseeded and the vineyards unpruned every
   seven years. The cancellation of debts and the freeing of slaves
   every seventh year reminded the Israelites of their deliverance from
   Egypt (Ex. 21:2-6; Deut. 15:12-18; cf. Heb. 4:1-11).
4. *Year of Jubilee*—after seven observances of the Sabbatical year
   came the year of Jubilee. This marked the year of liberty in which
   family inheritance was restored to those who had the misfortune
   of losing it, Hebrew slaves were freed, and the land was left un-
   cultivated (Lev. 25:8-55; cf. Acts 4:36, 37; 11:29; I Cor. 7:23).
5. *Passover and Feast of Unleavened Bread*—first observed in Egypt
   and annually reminded each family of their deliverance from Egypt.
   The Passover was the principal event, followed by a week when
   only unleavened bread was eaten. The Passover was observed on
   the fourteenth day of Nisan, the seventh month of their civil year,
   but the first month of their religious year (Ex. 34:17, 18; Deut.
   16:1-7; cf. Matt. 26:26-29; Luke 22:7-11; 12:1; I Cor. 5:6-8).
6. *Feast of Weeks*—observed 50 days after the Passover. Offerings on
   this day consisted of grain or flour, acknowledging that their daily
   bread was provided by God (Lev. 23:15-20; cf. Acts 1:5; 2:1).
7. *Feast of Tabernacles*—the final festival of the religious year held
   at the end of the harvest season. By living in booths during this
   week, they were to remind themselves of their wilderness sojourn.
   Every seven years at this time the Law was read publicly (Deut.
   31:9-13; cf. John 7:2).
8. *Day of Atonement*—the most solemn observance during the entire
   year (Lev. 16:1-34; 23:26-32; Num. 29:7-11; cf. Heb. 7:27).

The instructions given to the Israelites at Mount Sinai made it possible
for them to adopt a pattern of living that would distinguish them from
the heathen environment in Egypt as well as Canaan. The Law, the

tabernacle, the priesthood, the offerings, and the feasts and seasons were provisions and means for them to live in conformity to God's plan for His covenant people. Obedience and faith were essential in maintaining this covenant relationship.

Guide Questions for Study and Discussion

1. Give the major movements of Exodus—Deuteronomy as outlined in the text.
2. Why did Pharaoh intensify the oppression of Israel?
3. What training did Moses receive in the desert which helped prepare him for future leadership?
4. What problems did Moses present to God as objections to His call?
5. What answers did God give to assure Moses?
6. What was the purpose of the plagues?
7. What plague climaxed the contest between Pharaoh and God?
8. What was the condition of Israel's covenant relationship with God (cf. Ex. 19:1-5)?
9. How did Israel differ from the Egyptians in their worship of God?

Activities for Enrichment and Application

1. Trace the supernatural events throughout Exodus which made the Israelites aware of God's interest and care. What part does the supernatural play in God's manifestation of His concern for His people today?
2. With a concordance, trace the use of the word *passover* throughout the Scriptures. Why is this event given such prominence? In what way is the Lord's Supper a comparable Christian activity?
3. Make a simple diagram of the tabernacle and its court, indicating the furniture in each part. Indicate possible symbolic teaching found in the tabernacle and its furnishings (Ex. 25—28; 35—40).
4. Show how the feasts, offerings, and priesthood aided the Israelites in serving God. How did these point to the redemptive work of Christ?
5. Show how the plagues were related to the gods of Egypt.

Significant Resources

ALLIS, OSWALD T. "Leviticus" in *The New Bible Commentary: Revised*. Ed. by D. Guthrie, J. A. Moyter, A. M. Stibbs, and D. J. Wiseman. Grand Rapids: Wm. B. Eerdmans Pub. Co., 1970.
FREE, JOSEPH P. *Archaeology and Bible History*. Wheaton, IL: Scripture Press, 1976.
HARRISON, R. K. *Old Testament Times*. Grand Rapids: Wm. B. Eerdmans Pub. Co., 1970.
KEIL, CARL F., & DELITZSCH, FRANTZ. *Commentary on the Old Testament*. Vol. II. Grand Rapids: Wm. B. Eerdmans Pub Co., 1949.
MACKINTOSH, C. H. *Genesis to Deuteronomy: Notes on the Pentateuch*. New York: Loizeaux Bros., 1972.
SCHULTZ, SAMUEL J. *Gospel of Moses*. New York: Harper & Row, 1974.

CHAPTER FOUR

Looking Forward to Canaan

SCRIPTURE SURVEY: Numbers—Deuteronomy

EXTENT OF TIME: ca. 1600-1400 B.C.

Israel's encampment in the environs of Mount Sinai lasted for nearly one year. While there, additional instructions were given to the new nation. These are recorded in the first part of the book of Numbers. After an eleven-day march to Kadesh, spies were sent into Canaan which precipitated a crisis and the divine verdict that prolonged the wanderings. Thirty-eight years later they proceeded to the Plains of Moab where Moses gave his farewell speeches as found in the book of Deuteronomy.

ORGANIZATION Detailed instructions regarding organization for their
OF ISRAEL encampment and journey are summarized in Numbers. These chapters are not necessarily in chronological order. They may be outlined as follows:

I. Numbering Israel   Numbers 1:1—4:49
    A. Military census, 1:1-54
    B. Camp assignments, 2:1-34
    C. Levites and their duties, 3:1—4:49
II. Camp Regulations   5:1—6:21
    A. Restrictions of evil practices, 5:1-31
    B. Nazarite vows, 6:1-21
III. Religious Life of Israel   6:22—9:14
    A. Tabernacle worship instituted, 6:22—8:26
    B. The second Passover, 9:1-14
IV. Provisions for Guidance   9:15—10:10
    A. Divine manifestations, 9:15-23
    B. Human responsibility, 10:1-10

Israel was numbered before leaving Mount Sinai. Very likely this census also represented a tabulation of the count taken when they left Egypt a year earlier (Ex. 30:11 ff.; 38:26). Excluding women, children, and the Levites, the count was about 600,000. Almost forty years later after the rebellious generation had perished in the wilderness, their manpower was approximately the same (Num. 26).

A. Marching order

Law and order were essential for God's people. The Levites were

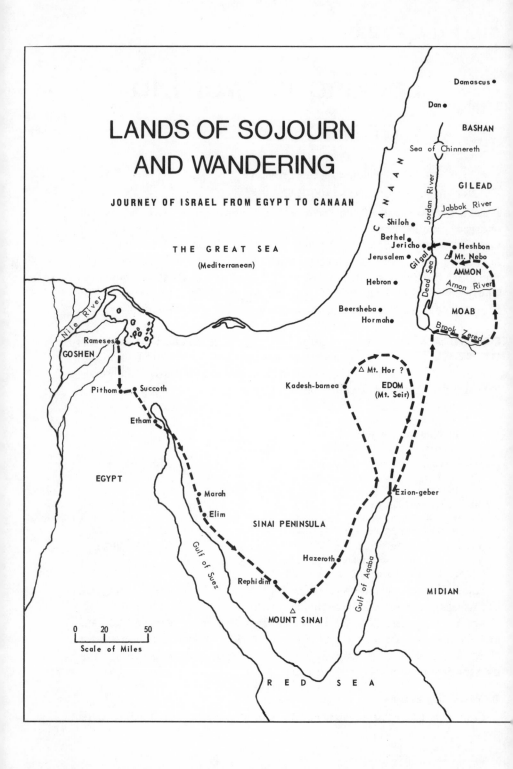

LANDS OF SOJOURN
AND WANDERING

JOURNEY OF ISRAEL FROM EGYPT TO CANAAN

THE GREAT SEA

(Mediterranean)

Damascus ●

Dan ●

BASHAN

Sea of Chinnereth

C A N A A N

Jordan River

GILEAD

Jabbok River

Shiloh ●

Bethel ●
Jericho ●
Jerusalem ●

Gilgal

Heshbon ●
△ Mt. Nebo

AMMON

Hebron ●

Arnon River

Beersheba ●
Hormah ●

Dead Sea

MOAB

Brook Zered

Nile River

○

Rameses ●

GOSHEN

Pithom ● ● Succoth

Etham ●

EGYPT

Marah ●

Elim ●

SINAI PENINSULA

Gulf of Suez

Rephidim ●

△
MOUNT SINAI

Hazeroth ●

Gulf of Aqaba

△ Mt. Hor ?

Kadesh-barnea ●

EDOM
(Mt. Seir)

Ezion-geber ●

MIDIAN

0   20   50
Scale of Miles

R E D   S E A

substituted for the firstborn of each family and assigned to care for the tabernacle. In the camp of Israel the tabernacle was in the center with the Levites surrounding the tabernacle and three tribes in each direction beyond the Levites. When en route, six tribes preceded the Levites who carried the tabernacle and six tribes followed.

B. Tabernacle dedicated

Impressive in the memory of the Israelites must have been the events during the first month of the second year after they left Egypt. The tabernacle with all its furnishings had been completed and erected. With Moses officiating, the tabernacle was dedicated and became the center of Israel's religious life (Ex. 40:1-3; Num. 6:22—9:14). Offerings were presented, Aaron and the Levites were publicly presented and dedicated for their services, and the congregation was divinely blessed with these words:

The Lord bless thee and keep thee:

The Lord make his face to shine upon thee, and be gracious unto thee:

The Lord lift up his countenance upon thee, and give thee peace (Num. 6:24-27).

The observance of the Passover marked their first anniversary of deliverance from Egypt. Special emphasis was given that everyone, even strangers, should participate.

C. On to Canaan

On the twentieth day of the second month the Israelites were alerted to break up camp in preparing for their journey to Canaan. Divine guidance was provided in the pillar of cloud by day and the pillar of fire by night. Observe carefully the importance of divine guidance, as well as the requirement for efficient organization and procedure. Proper coordination of the human and divine are exemplified in these instructions for Israel and deserve consideration and application for the mission of the Church today.

WILDERNESS WANDERINGS Israel's movement from Mount Sinai to the Plains of Moab is briefly summarized in Numbers 10:11—22:1. Comparatively little is known about the thirty-eight years they spent in wilderness wanderings as may be observed in the outline below:

I. From Mount Sinai to Kadesh   Numbers 10:11—12:16
 A. Order of procedure, 10:11-35
 B. Murmurings and judgments, 11:1—12:16
II. The Kadesh Crisis   13:1—14:45
 A. The spies and their reports, 13:1-33
 B. Rebellion and judgment, 14:1-45

III. The Years of Wandering   15:1—19:22
   A. Laws—future and present, 15:1-41
   B. The great rebellion, 16:1-50
   C. Vindication of appointed leaders, 17:1—19:22
IV. From Kadesh to the Plains of Moab   20:1—22:1
   A. Death of Miriam, 20:1
   B. Sins of Moses and Aaron, 20:2-13
   C. Edom refuses Israel passage, 20:14-21
   D. Death of Aaron, 20:22-29
   E. Israel avenges defeat by Canaanites, 21:1-3
   F. The brazen serpent, 21:4-9
   G. March around Moab, 21:10-20
   H. Defeat of Sihon and Og, 21:21-35
   I. Arrival on the Plains of Moab, 22:1.

En route to Kadesh the Israelites complained and rebelled. Seventy elders were appointed to share responsibility with Moses in controlling the people as they murmured about the manna. When an abundant supply of quail was divinely provided, the people were so intemperate and indulgent that many died in the resultant plague. Even Aaron and Miriam complained against Moses whom God vindicated as leader.

A. The Kadesh crisis

Spies were sent into the land of Canaan as Israel moved north to encamp at Kadesh, approximately forty miles south and somewhat west of Beersheba. The twelve men unanimously reported both the excellency of the land and the potential strength and ferocity of the inhabitants. But as to the prospects for conquest they were not agreed. Ten declared that occupation was impossible and stirred up public sentiment for an immediate return to Egypt. Two—Joshua and Caleb—confidently asserted that with divine aid conquest was possible. The people were swayed by the majority's report and became an insolent mob, threatening to stone Joshua and Caleb, and even considered selecting a new leader to replace Moses.

Divine judgment followed. This generation which less than two years before had seen God's mighty acts in delivering them from the clutches of Pharaoh should have had enough evidence to believe that God would aid them in the conquest of Canaan. When God contemplated annihilation, Moses intervened. Even though pardon was extended to the nation, the ten spies and all people aged twenty and older were consigned to death in the wilderness because of their lack of faith.

B. The years of wandering

The great rebellion led by Korah, Dathan, and Abiram represents two mutinous groups, mutually strengthened through their cooperative effort (Num. 16:1-50).[1] Korah and his supporting Levites challenged the

---
[1] For a detailed analysis, see A. A. MacRae, "Numbers," in the *New Bible Commentary* (Grand Rapids: Wm. B. Eerdmans Pub. Co., 1953), pp. 162-194.

leadership of Aaron and his family who were responsible for the priestly ministry in Israel. Dathan and Abiram aspired to replace Moses as political leader, since they were the descendants of Reuben the oldest son of Jacob. Both Moses and Aaron were vindicated when the earth swallowed up Dathan and Abiram and their families and Korah.[2] Before this rebellion completely subsided, more than 14,000 people had perished in the camp of Israel. Aaron's place as priest was also confirmed by the miraculous sign of the budding rod.

C. En route to the Plains of Moab

After marking time for approximately thirty-eight years in the area of Kadesh—a time during which many more murmurings and rebellions may have occurred than are recorded here—Israel was led by the way of the Gulf of Aqaba to the Plains of Moab. Among the numerous events along the way, it is significant to note that Moses in response to the complaints of the Israelites became irate and impatient. For his disobedience in smiting the rock instead of commanding it to bring forth water, Moses was denied the privilege of entering Canaan. The experience of the Israelites when punished by a scourge of serpents is also significant. Through simple obedience and faith, those who looked at the bronze serpent erected by Moses were saved. The Lord Jesus used this incident as a symbol of His death on the cross, applying the same principle—anyone who turned to Him would not perish but have eternal life (John 3:14-16).

By moving southward, the Israelites circumvented Edom and later Moab as they settled in the plains north of the Arnon River and east of the Dead Sea. Although forbidden to fight against Moab, the Israelites fought against Sihon, king of Heshbon, and Og, the king of Bashan, as they occupied this land north of Moab.

INSTRUCTIONS FOR ENTERING CANAAN The experiences and instructions that came to Israel while encamped on the Plains of Moab conditioned God's holy nation for possessing the land of promise. A brief survey of these developments is provided in the following outline:

I. Preservation of God's Chosen People   Numbers 22:2—25:18
   A. Balak's design to curse Israel, 22:2-40
   B. Balaam's blessings, 22:41—24:24
   C. Seduction and judgment, 24:25—25:18
II. Preparation for Conquest   26:1—33:49
   A. The new generation, 26:1-65
   B. Inheritance problems, 27:1-11

---

[2] Korah's family did not perish. His descendants occupy an honored place in subsequent history. Samuel ranks perhaps next to Moses as a great prophet. Heman, a grandson of Samuel, was an outstanding singer in David's time. A number of psalms are designated as "for the sons of Korah."

C. A new leader, 27:12-23
D. Sacrifices and vows, 28:1—30:16
E. Vengeance on the Midianites, 31:1-54
F. Transjordan apportioned, 32:1-42
G. Review of Israel's journey, 33:1-49
III. Anticipation of Occupation   33:50—36:13
    A. The land to be conquered, 33:50—34:15
    B. Leaders appointed for allotting
       the land, 34:16-29
    C. Levitical and refuge cities, 35:1-34
    D. Inheritance regulations, 36:1-13

A. Balaam and Balak

King Balak of the Moabites was disturbed when the Israelites encamped to the north of him. He endeavored to persuade Balaam to come to his aid, hoping that this prophet would curse Israel. Enticed by the reward offered, Balaam went but was shockingly reminded by his donkey and the angel that he was limited in this mission to speak God's message only. Four times Balaam blessed Israel and subsequently was shamefully dismissed by Balak. However, through Balaam's advice (Num. 31:16), the Moabites seduced many Israelites into immorality and idolatry which brought judgment upon God's people. Balaam was killed in a battle between the Israelites and Midianites. God, however, would not allow His people to be cursed.

B. Decisions and instructions

The territory east of Jordan appealed to the Reubenites and Gadites as excellent grazing land. In response, Moses reluctantly granted permission to Reuben, Gad, and half the tribe of Manasseh to settle east of the Jordan but exacted a promise from them to participate in the conquest of Canaan. Three cities of refuge were appointed in this territory.

Most significant among other instructions and plans outlined by Moses was the designation of Joshua as the new leader (Num. 27). He had already distinguished himself as a military leader when they repulsed the Amalekites (Ex. 17), and as a man of faith when he was sent in to spy out the land.

RETROSPECT Moses' ministry was nearing completion. In the wake **AND PROSPECT** of new leadership and conquest and occupation of the promised land, Moses addressed the nation he had led out of Egypt in a number of public addresses. They may be considered under the following divisions:

I. History and Its Significance   Deuteronomy 1:1—4:43
    A. Review of Israel's failures, 1:1—3:29
    B. Admonition to obedience, 4:1-40

C. Transjordan cities and refuge, 4:41-43
II. The Law and Its Significance   4:44—28:68
    A. The covenant and the Decalogue, 4:44—11:32
    B. Laws for living in Canaan, 12:1—26:19
    C. Blessings and curses, 27:1—28:68
III. Final Preparation and Farewell   29:1—34:12
    A. Israel's choice of blessing or curse, 29:1—30:20
    B. Joshua commissioned, 31:1-29
    C. The song and blessing of Moses, 31:30—33:29
    D. The death of Moses, 34:1-12

Vital and significant were the messages Moses delivered to his people. No one knew the Israelites any better than Moses, nor was anyone else in a better position to anticipate the future developments.

A. History

In his first address Moses reviewed Israel's history. He began with their encampment and departure in the Sinai Peninsula. He highlighted this review by reminding them that the generation that came out of Egypt murmured and rebelled repeatedly and in consequence was denied entrance into the land of promise. Clearly and distinctly he pointed out that the conditions for obtaining God's favor were obedience to the Law and a wholehearted devotion to God.

B. Law

In his second address Moses vividly reminded them that they were God's covenant people. He repeated the Ten Commandments and pointed out that these were basic to a life acceptable to God. Genuine love for God would issue in a life of obedience which would maintain them as God's holy people in the midst of pagan surroundings. Idolatry together with idolatrous people were to be removed. Moses also set forth rules and ordinances to guide them in their civil, social, and domestic responsibilities. The blessings and curses outlined by Moses were to be read publicly to the entire congregation after they entered Canaan.

C. Farewell

When Moses resigned, he entrusted Joshua with the leadership and the priests with his teaching ministry. He provided them with a copy of the Law. How complete this copy was is not indicated but it was stored with the ark, making it available to be read publicly to the congregation every seven years according to provisions previously made. Moses once more recounted the birth and childhood of the nation that he had led from Egyptian slavery to the border of Canaan and uttered a blessing for each tribe. Before he died, Moses was instructed to ascend Mount Nebo from which he viewed the land the Israelites were about to enter.

Guide Questions for Study and Discussion

1. What was the population count of Israel before they left Mount Sinai?
2. How did the Israelites celebrate their first anniversary after the Exodus?
3. Where was the tabernacle located when Israel was encamped or en route?
4. What precipitated the crisis causing Israel to remain in the wilderness for an extended period?
5. How did Joshua and Caleb propose the conquest of Canaan?
6. Who were the leaders of two rebellions against Moses and Aaron?
7. How is the incident of the serpent used in the New Testament?
8. What nation refused to let Israel use their highway?
9. Who was Balak?
10. Why was Moses denied entrance into Canaan?

Activities for Enrichment and Application

1. Trace the movement of Israel from Mount Sinai to the Plains of Moab via Kadesh-barnea. What spiritual lessons still applicable should have been learned as the result of these travels?
2. Study the means of guidance provided through the pillar of cloud and the trumpets in Numbers 10. What means does God use to guide His children today?
3. Point out how Deuteronomy 4—6 can be helpful to parents in rearing their children. Discuss practical ways to apply Deuteronomy 6:7 in family life.
4. Evaluate the character of Balaam as a prophet of God. Does God use similar individuals today?

Significant Resources

AHARONI, Y., AND AVI-YONAH, The Macmillan Bible Atlas. New York: Macmillan Pub. Co., 1977.

PFEIFFER, CHARLES F. The Bible Atlas. Rev. ed. Nashville: Broadman Press, 1973.

SCHULTZ, SAMUEL J. Deuteronomy—The Gospel of Love. Chicago: Moody Press, 1971.

SMICK, ELMER. "Numbers" in Wycliffe Bible Commentary. Ed. by Charles F. Pfeiffer & Everett F. Harrison. Chicago: Moody Press, 1962.

CHAPTER FIVE

Possessing the Promised Land

SCRIPTURE SURVEY: Joshua, Judges, Ruth

EXTENT OF TIME: ca. 1400-1100 B.C.

From their encampment northeast of the Dead Sea, the Israelites could view the land of Canaan across the River Jordan. Before Moses died, Joshua had been appointed to lead them in conquest and occupation.

CONDITIONS IN CANAAN Politically, the land was under the control of people who lived in city-states. A walled city situated on top of a mound could resist an invading force for almost an indefinite period as long as their water and food supply lasted. Consequently, for Israel conquest and occupation seemed like a formidable and impossible assignment.

The Canaanites were polytheistic in their religion. El was the chief god who was called "father bull" and creator. His wife's name was Asherah. Chief among their many offspring was Baal, meaning "lord" (I Kings 18:19). He was the reigning king of the gods who were believed to control heaven and earth and fertility.

The brutality and immorality in the stories of these gods were unsurpassed in our present knowledge of Near Eastern gods during that period. This lack of morality was reflected in the religious rites and ceremonies of the Canaanites. Archaeologists have pointed out that the evidence of Canaanite culture of Joshua's time indicates that the people practiced child sacrifice, religious prostitution, and snake worship in their religious rites and ceremonies.[1] The conditions, however, were known to Moses and he warned the Israelites that if they did not destroy these wicked people, the Israelites would be ensnared in the sins of the Canaanites (Lev. 18:24-28; 20—23; Deut. 12:31; 20:17, 18).

This divine judgment coming upon the Canaanites through the Israelites was preceded by a long period of mercy. The patriarchs while living in Canaan had erected their altars in numerous places, exemplifying the worship of the true God of heaven and earth. When God promised

---

[1] G. Ernest Wright and Floyd V. Filson, eds. *Westminster Historical Atlas of the Bible* (Philadelphia: Westminster Press, 1956), p. 34.

Abraham the land of Canaan for his descendants (Gen. 15:16), the Bible states that the iniquity of the Amorite was not yet full and that the Israelites would dwell in Egypt for four centuries. After this long period, the Canaanites had become worse so that the time for judgment was ripe as Israel entered to occupy the land.

THE CONQUEST   Joshua came to this responsible position of leadership
UNDER JOSHUA   with a background of experience and training under
                    Moses' tutelage. At Rephidim (in the wilderness)
Joshua led the Israelites in victory, repulsing the Amalekite attack (Ex. 17:8-16) as Moses continued in intercessory prayer for him. As a spy he gained firsthand knowledge of Palestine and heroically, in face of opposition, asserted that by faith in God they would be able to conquer the land (Num. 13, 14). Thus he had witnessed God's power exercised in their behalf from Egypt to the borders of Canaan, even though an entire generation was denied the privilege of entrance because of unbelief.

A. Entrance into Canaan

In the first four chapters are narrated the events of Israel's movement into Palestine. These may be outlined as follows:

I. Joshua Assumes Leadership	Joshua 1
II. Two Spies Sent to Jericho	2
III. Passage through the Jordan	3
IV. Memorials	4

Joshua was assured of success if he would be careful to heed the instructions given in the book of the Law which had been given through Moses. Under God's command and with assurance of God's presence, he assumed this task of leading God's chosen nation. Two spies who were sent to Jericho learned from Rahab that the stories of God's mighty acts in behalf of Israel were circulating among the inhabitants of Canaan.

The miraculous passage through the Jordan should have made every Israelite of this new generation conscious of God's intervention for them. Provision was made by erecting two twelve-stone memorials—one in or near the Jordan and another at Gilgal—to remind coming generations of this great event.

B. The major campaigns

In six chapters the summary of Joshua's campaigns is given. Note the following developments:

I. Preparation for the Campaigns	Joshua 5
II. Central Campaign—Jericho and Ai	6
III. Southern Campaign—Amorite League	9
IV. Northern Campaign—Canaanite League	11:1-15
V. Tabulation of the Conquest	11:16—12:24

Four events made the whole nation of Israel conscious of the fact that they were in the land of promise:

1. They erected two memorials of stones to perpetuate the memory of divine deliverance.
2. They observed the Passover, reminding the new generation of their deliverance from Egypt.
3. They observed the rite of circumcision, making them conscious of the fact that they were God's covenant people.
4. Manna ceased and their sustenance came from the land which they had entered.

In addition, Joshua was personally reminded through a theophany (a physical manifestation of God) that he was but a servant and subject to the Commander of the army of the Lord (5:13-15).

The central campaign was directed against Jericho and Ai. The former was a sample victory, making all Israel aware of God's supernatural power released in their behalf. Peculiar to this victory was the fact that the Israelites were not allowed to retain any spoils of conquest. (Ai was conquered according to regular military strategy after Achan's sin had been removed.) After this victory the Israelites were allowed the livestock and other property.[2] Following the occupation of central Canaan, the Israelites assembled between Mount Ebal and Mount Gerizim for a convocation to hear the reading of the Law of Moses.

In the southern campaign the Amorite League was defeated. Through deception and insensitivity to divine guidance, the Israelites entered into a league with the Gibeonites. In consequence, the other cities of this league attacked Israel but through the divine intervention of hailstones, in addition to a surprise counter attack and extension of daylight, the Israelites were able to rout the enemy in a smashing victory.[3] Although such city-states as Gezer and Jerusalem were not conquered, the whole area from Gibeon down to Kadesh-barnea was under the control of Joshua.

The northern campaign is briefly described. In a great battle near the waters of Merom, the Canaanites were defeated. The city of Hazor was utterly destroyed. Recent excavation under the Israeli expedition begun in 1955 indicate that this Canaanite city may have had a population of over 40,000 at this time.

In summary, thirty-one kings are listed as having been defeated in the conquest of Canaan. Although the inhabitants of Canaan were not

---

[2] For a discussion of the possibility that the city of Bethel was included in this conquest, see Schultz, *The Old Testament Speaks*, p. 97.

[3] For various views and interpretations of this miracle of Joshua's long day, see Bernard Ramm, *The Christian View of Science and Scripture* (Grand Rapids: Wm. B. Eerdmans Pub. Co., 1955), pp. 156-161.

destroyed as extensively as Moses had instructed the Israelites, Joshua was able to allot the land.

C. Division of the land

The remaining chapters of Joshua describe the allotment of the promised land and the farewell advice of Joshua as follows:

I. Plan for Division	Joshua 13—14
II. Tribal Allotment	15—19
III. Refuge and Levite Cities	20—21
IV. Farewell and Death of Joshua	22—24

After tribal boundaries were established, six cities were designated as cities of refuge—three on each side of the Jordan River. Forty-eight cities were assigned to the Levites who were scattered throughout the land in order to meet their responsibilities in religious service. Shiloh was designated as the religious center of Israel. Here the tabernacle was erected (Josh. 1:18). Before Joshua died, he assembled the Israelites at Shechem, reminding them that Abraham had been called from idolatry and admonishing them to fear the Lord.

LEADERSHIP OF JUDGES The events in Joshua and Judges are closely related. The exact chronology of this era is very difficult to establish but for approximately two or three centuries the destiny of Israel is surveyed under the leadership of judges who rose to deliver their people from the oppressing enemies. Most of these leaders ruled locally and, consequently, the years allotted to each may have been synchronous with the preceding or succeeding judge.

A. Prevailing conditions

A general description of the times of the judges is given in the opening chapters of Judges as follows:

I. Unoccupied Areas	Judges 1:1—2:5
II. Religious-Political Cycles	2:6—3:6

Throughout the land, Canaanites had retained strongholds during Israel's conquest and occupation. As a result, the Israelites encountered continual difficulties, even though at times the inhabitants of such city-states as Jerusalem, Megiddo, Taanach, and others were subjected to hard labor and taxes. In days of Israel's spasmodic leadership, these heathen peoples gained the upper hand.

Fourfold cycles occurred repeatedly in Israel. Association with the pagan population led the Israelites into apostasy and idolatry. Judgment followed in the form of oppression by invading nations. In the course of time, the Israelites repented which resulted in divine deliverance. The

---

⁴ For a discussion of the chronology for this period, see Schultz, *op. cit.*, pp. 103-105.

religious-political cycles may also be characterized by the following words: sin, sorrow, supplication, and salvation.

B. Oppressing nations and deliverers

The history of Israel during this period is recorded with special interest in the oppressing nations and the judges that were raised to free the people from the invaders. Below is a list as given in Judges:

I. Mesopotamia—Othniel	Judges 3:7-11
II. Moab—Ehud	3:12-30
III. Philistia—Shamgar	3:31
IV. Canaan (Hazor)—Deborah and Barak	4:1—5:31
V. Midian—Gideon (Jerubbaal)	6:1—8:35
VI. Abimelech, Tola, and Jair	9:1—10:5
VII. Ammon—Jephthah	10:6—12:7
VIII. Ibzan, Elon, and Abdon	12:8-15
IX. Philistia—Samson	13:1—16:31

Most of these individuals apparently performed great feats in behalf of the Israelites, even though some of them are only mentioned by name. The oppressing nations came from the neighboring territories gradually invading various areas of tribal possessions, taking their crops, and occupying the land. Some of these nations would exact taxes that became a terrible burden to the Israelites.

The stories of a number of these judges deserve careful study. Five of them—Barak, Gideon, Jephthah, Samson, and Samuel—are listed among the heroes of faith in Hebrews chapter 11. Individual deeds and battles exhibiting supernatural strength restored to the Israelites the consciousness that God was intervening in behalf of His people. Some of the judges are merely mentioned by name, with very little information given concerning their activities.

C. Confused conditions

The last five chapters of the book of Judges and the four chapters of the book of Ruth relate the blessings and adversities of various groups and families. These may be briefly outlined as follows:

I. Micah and His Idolatry	Judges 17
II. Migration of the Danites	18
III. Crime and Civil War	19—21
IV. The Story of Ruth	Ruth 1—4

Historical details in these chapters are lacking so that at best these events can be dated in the days "when the judges ruled," and there was "no king in Israel" (Ruth 1:1; Judg. 21:25). Certainly the national developments are not given and the statement "Every man did that which was right in his own eyes" (Judg. 21:25) characterized the plight of Israel during the times of the judges.

Guide Questions for Study and Discussion

1. *What were the conditions for Joshua's success?
2. How were future generations to be reminded of Israel's crossing the Jordan?
3. What did Rahab know about Israel when she conversed with the spies?
4. How did Israel observe its entrance into Canaan?
5. Why were the Israelites forbidden to take any spoils after the fall of Jericho?
6. Where did Joshua assemble the people for the reading of the Law of Moses?
7. How did the Gibeonites deceive Joshua?
8. Where did the Levites live in Canaan?
9. What judges are listed in Hebrews 11?
10. What were the prevailing religious-political conditions during the time of the judges?

Activities for Enrichment and Application

1. Trace the major events in the conquest of the land of Canaan. In each instance indicate the determining factors for victory or defeat. Which of these factors are significant in Christian experience? (Cf. Rom. 6—8; Eph. 1—6.)
2. Locate on a map the five cities conquered in the southern campaign. To what degree did divine intervention utilize physical factors in giving success?
3. What characteristics and abilities seen in Joshua's leadership are essential to effective Christian leadership?
4. How does the story of Ruth illustrate the truth that God has never left Himself without witness? How does this account advance the Messianic hope?

Significant Resources

EDERSHEIM, ALFRED. Old Testament Bible History. 1954. Reprint. Grand Rapids: Wm. B. Eerdmans Pub. Co., 1972.

FREE, JOSEPH P. Archaeology and Bible History. Wheaton, IL: Scripture Press, 1976.

PAYNE, J. BARTON. "Joshua" in The New Pictorial Bible Dictionary. Ed. by Merrill C. Tenney. Grand Rapids: Zondervan Pub. House, 1963.

———. "Book of Judges" in The New Bible Dictionary. Ed. by J. D. Douglas. Grand Rapids: Wm. B. Eerdmans Pub. Co., 1962.

CHAPTER SIX

Time of Transition

SCRIPTURE SURVEY: I Samuel

EXTENT OF TIME: ca. 1100-1000 B.C.

Crucial was the threat of Philistine supremacy over Israel. Settled in the maritime plain in the southwestern part of Palestine, the Philistines began to overrun the Israelites in the days of Samson. With the Israelites lacking centralized national leadership, they failed in repulsing the Philistines. Even though Samson was endowed with supernatural power, he failed to use this to the best advantage of Israel's national interest.

Philistine superiority over Israel is best explained by the fact that they held the secrets in smelting iron. Although the Hittites in Asia Minor had been iron founders before 1200 B.C., the Philistines were the first to use this process in Palestine. They guarded this monopoly carefully and as a result held Israel at their mercy. "There was no smith found throughout all the land of Israel" (I Sam. 13:19-22). As a result the Israelites were dependent upon the Philistines for the production of spears and swords as well as the sharpening of their farm implements.

Politically the Philistines occupied at least five cities in the maritime plain which were independently ruled by a "lord." The names of these cities—Ashkelon, Ashdod, Ekron, Gaza, and Gath—appear in the biblical records.

The Scriptures reflect this struggle between the Philistines and the Israelites during several generations. Under the leadership of Eli, Samuel, and Saul, the tribes of Israel were united to some extent in their resistance against the Philistines. There were times when it seemed as though the Israelites were on the verge of being subjected to hopeless slavery. By about 1000 B.C. under David the power of the Philistines was broken.

ELI AS PRIEST AND JUDGE The events related in I Samuel 1—4 occurred during the days of Eli's leadership. They may be briefly outlined as follows:

I. Birth of Samuel	I Samuel 1:1—2:11
II. Tabernacle Service	2:12-26
III. Two Warnings to Eli	2:27—3:21
IV. Judgment on Eli	4:1-22

Shiloh, where the tabernacle was erected in the days of Joshua (Josh.

18:1), apparently continued to be Israel's religious center. Here Eli served as high priest and provided religious and civil leadership for the people. Although the narrative already is focused upon Samuel, the conditions existing during the days of Eli are vividly portrayed.

A. Religious apostasy

The religion of Israel was at an all-time low when Eli was in charge. He failed to teach his sons to revere God as Moses had clearly instructed Israelite parents to do (Deut. 4—6). Of Eli's sons, Hophni and Phinehas, it is said that "they knew not the Lord" (I Sam. 2:12). Nevertheless, they were allowed to assume priestly responsibilities, taking advantage of the people as they came to sacrifice and worship. Not only did they rob God in demanding the priestly portion before sacrifice was made, but they conducted themselves in such a manner that the people abhorred bringing their sacrifices to Shiloh. They profaned the sanctuary with the baseness and debauchery common in Canaanite religion. Consequently, it is not surprising that Israel continued to degenerate into increasingly corrupt religious practices.

This religious atmosphere in Shiloh was the environment to which Samuel was exposed as a growing child. Transferred from the care of a God-fearing mother, Samuel was subjected to the evil degrading influences of the sons of the high priest in the national religious center. It was to the benefit of Israel that Samuel reacted against this godless pressure and became conscious of God's call in the early years of his life.

B. Impending judgment

The laxity of Eli provoked God's judgment. Twice he was warned. An unnamed prophet clearly pointed out to Eli that he was honoring his sons more than he honored God (I Sam. 2:30). His lack of parental discipline extended to his priestly office as the sons assumed responsibilities at the tabernacle. With the call of Samuel, a second message of warning was conveyed to Eli (I Sam. 3).

The day of judgment affected the entire nation. In the course of a battle against the Philistines, the sons of Eli yielded to the pressure of the people to take the ark of the covenant out of the Holy of Holies in the tabernacle and bring it into the battlefield, hoping this would force God to give them victory.

The defeat of Israel was crushing. The ark was stolen, the sons of Eli were slain, and the report of these reverses for Israel shocked Eli so that he collapsed and died. In all likelihood, Shiloh was destroyed. When the ark was returned, it was placed in a private home. No mention is made of Shiloh or the tabernacle. Shortly after this, priests officiated at Nob (I Sam. 21:1).

So demoralizing was this defeat of Israel that when Eli's daughter-in-law gave birth to a son she named him "Ichabod" because she sensed that God's blessing had been withdrawn from Israel.

SAMUEL AS PROPHET, Brief but significant are the chapters in I Sam-
PRIEST, AND JUDGE uel that project the religious and political changes that took place under the leadership of Samuel. Consider the following outline:

I. The Ark Restored to Israel	I Samuel 5:1—7:2	
II. Revival and Victory	7:3-14	
III. Summary of Samuel's Ministry	7:15—8:3	
IV. Request for a King	8:4-22	
V. Saul Anointed	9:1—10:16	
VI. Public Acclaim and Victory	10:17—11:11	
VII. Saul's Inauguration; Samuel's Pledge	11:12—12:25	

Samuel has a unique place in Israel's history. He was the last of the judges who exercised civil jurisdiction over Israel in that capacity. Although he was not of the lineage of Aaron, he officiated as the leading priest. He also gained renown as a prophet and established schools of the prophets who influenced the kings of Israel in succeeding generations.

A. Effective leadership

Samuel erected an altar in his home town of Ramah. Although the ark was returned, it was stored in the home of Abinadab until the time of David. Samuel established circuits throughout Israel in performing his priestly duties and effective teaching ministry. Places mentioned in the Biblical account are: Mizpah, Ramah, Gilgal, Bethlehem, Bethel, and Beersheba. In the course of time, prophetic bands gathered about Samuel, as all Israel from Dan to Beersheba became conscious of the fact that he was established as a prophet of the Lord.

The purging of Canaanite cultic worship from the ranks of Israel was also effected under the influence of Samuel. When Samuel gathered the Israelites for a convocation of prayer, fasting, and sacrifice at Mizpah, the Philistines attacked. In the midst of the battle, the Philistines were confused and fled as a result of a severe thunderstorm. Samuel acknowledged God's help and intervention by erecting a stone which he named "Ebenezer" meaning "Hitherto hath the Lord helped us" (I Sam. 7:12). Not again did the Philistines attack the Israelites while Samuel was in charge of Israel.

B. Request for a king

Reluctantly, Samuel listened and finally consented to Israel's demand for a king. Samuel eloquently implored his people "not to impose upon themselves a Canaanite institution alien to their own way of life." Sensitive to divine guidance, Samuel agreed and turned the affairs of state over to a new leader (I Sam. 8:7-22).

SAUL ANOINTED AS Saul was God's choice to be Israel's first king **ISRAEL'S FIRST KING** after the people clamored for a leader like unto other nations. Saul was privately anointed and publicly acclaimed in a convocation at Mizpah, as the people enthusiastically shouted "Long live the king." The nature of kingship in Israel, however, was uniquely set forth in the statement that Saul was to be "captain of His (God's) inheritance" (I Sam. 9:16; 10:1).

The deliverance of Jabesh-gilead from the Ammonite threat under the leadership of Saul projected the new king into the national limelight. In a public meeting at Gilgal after this victory Samuel publicly endorsed Saul as king with the warning that prosperity was dependent upon the obedience of the king as well as his subjects to the Law of Moses. This message was confirmed by a sudden rain and thunder during the wheat harvest, about May 15 to June 15. This was considered as a miracle since normally Palestine has virtually no rain from April to October. Samuel, however, assured his people of his sincere interest in their future welfare in his public statement: "God forbid that I should sin against the Lord in ceasing to pray for you."

Saul's leadership of Israel is vividly and dramatically portrayed in the remaining chapters of I Samuel. For a survey account, we may divide this into three outline units as indicated in the following pages.

    I. Saul Fails to Wait for Samuel   I Samuel 13:1-15a
   II. Philistines Defeated at Michmash   13:15b—14:46
  III. Surrounding Nations Subdued   14:47-52
  IV. Disobedience in an Amalekite Victory   15:1-35

Saul led his nation in numerous military victories. On a hill three miles north of Jerusalem he established Gibeah as a strong palace-fort which apparently served as his capital while he was king of Israel. Saul routed the Philistines at Michmash and defeated numerous other nations in addition to the Amalekites (I Sam. 14:47, 48).

King Saul had numerous advantages in his favor as he assumed the kingship. He was successful as a military leader and gained the national acclaim of his people. He also had the spiritual support of the nationally-known prophet Samuel who assured the king as well as the people of intercessory prayer. Success and public acclaim, however, did not obscure the personal weaknesses in Saul's character. These became evident in his impatience to wait for Samuel at Gilgal where Saul assumed priestly duties, and his disobedience to God's command through the prophet to utterly destroy the Amalekites. Sternly, Samuel rebuked him in the warning that "to obey is better than sacrifice." In failing to recognize his sacred trust, Saul was reminded that he had forfeited the kingdom.

DAVID'S RISE TO David's anointing by Samuel was unknown to Saul.
NATIONAL FAME In this experience the prophet Samuel was taught the lesson that man is prone to look on the outward appearance but the Lord appraises the heart. David in his youthful days had extensive preparation. During this time, he not only learned how to play instruments, but also to develop his strength and ingenuity in fighting off lions and bears. At the same time, he learned to place his trust in God for divine aid. On an errand of serving his older brothers who were in the army, David heard Goliath challenging the Israelites. David reasoned that God would help him kill the giant. By killing Goliath, David suddenly gained national recognition. While David had been brought before the king on previous occasions as a musician to calm Saul's troubled spirit, he then served the royal court on a permanent basis.

Saul yielded to jealousy as David arose in national fame. When subtle schemes devised to ensnare David failed repeatedly, Saul began to persecute David. In the meantime, one of the noblest friendships in the Old Testament developed between Jonathan and David which made it possible for the latter to be constantly aware of the king's malicious designs. Eventually, David was forced to take refuge in the Judean desert. During the times that Saul pursued David and his men, David twice had the opportunity to take the king's life but always refrained, affirming that he would not touch the Lord's anointed.

The Philistine-Israelite conflict:

David's fear that Saul might overtake him unawares caused him to seek refuge in the land of the Philistines. During the last year and a half of Saul's reign, David was granted permission by Achish to reside in the Philistine city of Ziklag. He was denied, however, the privilege of joining the Philistines in their warfare against Saul.

When the Philistines faced the Israelite armies which were encamped on Mount Gilboa, Saul had more to fear than this enemy whom he had previously defeated. Samuel, long ago ignored by Saul, was not available for interview. Saul was panic-stricken as he turned to God and received no answer by dream, by Urim, or by prophet. In desperation he turned to spiritualistic mediums which he himself had banned in the past. As Samuel had predicted, Saul's life ended with dismal night as he renewed his encounter with the Philistines. The invaders won a decisive victory, gaining control of the fertile valley of Megiddo from the coast to the Jordan River and occupying numerous cities. Tragic was the termination of the reign of Israel's first king. Although God-chosen and anointed by the praying prophet Samuel, Saul failed to realize that obedience was essential in the sacred and unique trust afforded him by God—to be "captain over His inheritance" (I Sam. 10:1).

Guide Questions for Study and Discussion

1. How did the Philistines maintain temporal control over the Israelites?
2. How was Eli warned about his laxity in his home and his office?
3. Why was the ark not returned to Shiloh?
4. Why did Saul stop at the home of Samuel?
5. Why did the Israelites request a king?
6. What cities were included in Samuel's circuit as a judge and prophet?
7. What talent of David brought him before the king?
8. Who was David's closest friend in the royal family?
9. What was David's attitude toward Saul?
10. Where was Saul's life terminated?

Activities for Enrichment and Application

1. What evident qualities in Samuel's life are necessary for effective Christian leadership?
2. On a map of Palestine list the leading cities mentioned in I Samuel. What earlier and later events added to their historical significance?
3. Trace the steps in Saul's downfall. Which of these inevitably lead to spiritual difficulties?
4. What qualities evidenced in David's life are always commendable? What experiences of his life point to Christian experience in preparation for effective leadership?
5. Compare and contrast the qualities required for kingship in Israel with that in heathen nations.

Significant Resources

FREE, JOSEPH P. *Archaeology and Bible History.* Wheaton, IL: Scripture Press, 1976.
MARTIN, W. J. "Samuel" in *The New Bible Dictionary.* Ed. by J. D. Douglas. Grand Rapids: Wm. B. Eerdmans Pub. Co., 1962.
WRIGHT, GEORGE E. *Biblical Archaeology.* Philadelphia: Westminster Press, 1963.
YOUNG, EDWARD J. *My Servants the Prophets.* Grand Rapids: Wm. B. Eerdmans Pub. Co., 1952.

CHAPTER SEVEN

The Reign of David

SCRIPTURE SURVEY: II Samuel, I Chronicles
EXTENT OF TIME: ca. 1011-971 B.C.

David was the outstanding king in the entire history of Israel in Old Testament times. His reign represents the epitome of Israel's national achievements and is so recognized throughout the Holy Scriptures.

Politically and religiously, David distinguished himself as a great leader. He was successful in uniting the tribes of Israel into an effective union and extending its territory from the river of Egypt and the Gulf of Aqaba to the Phoenician coast and the land of Hamath. Through military success and friendly overtures, David gained for Israel international respect and recognition that remained unchallenged until the death of Solomon.

Religiously, David organized the priests and Levites for effective participation in the ritual and ceremonial activities of the entire nation. Even though he was denied the privilege of building the temple, David made elaborate preparation for its erection during the reign of Solomon.

Two books in the Old Testament report the account of David's reign. Second Samuel depicts the Davidic reign in great detail and provides an exclusive account of the sin, crime, and rebellion in the royal family. First Chronicles traces the genealogical background of the twelve tribes and focuses attention upon David as the first king of the ruling dynasty of Israel. Saul is hardly mentioned. Much attention is given to the political and religious organization of Israel and the extensive description of David's preparation for building the temple.

The outline of David's reign as given in this chapter represents a suggested chronological arrangement of the events as recorded in II Samuel and I Chronicles.

	II Samuel	I Chronicles
I. Genealogical Background		1—9
II. David Laments Saul's Death	1	10
III. Disintegration of Saul's Dynasty	2—4	

THE KING OF JUDAH Israel was in serious trouble when they lost their king and three of his sons in Saul's last battle with the Philistines. Abner, who had served as captain of Saul's

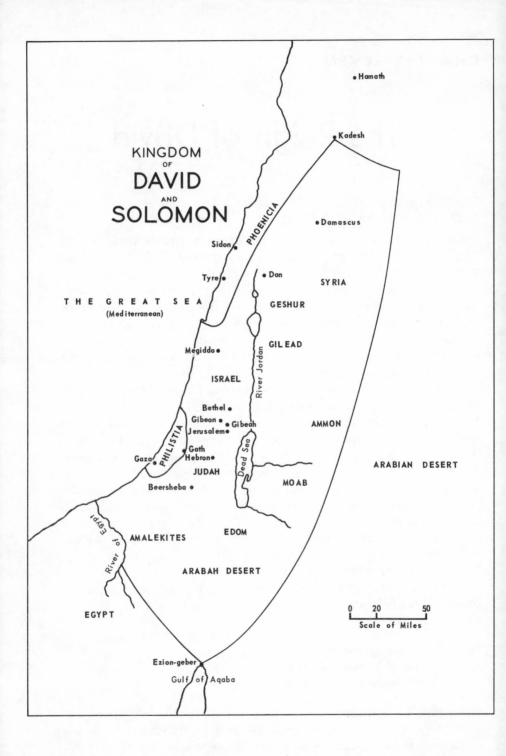

KINGDOM
OF
DAVID
AND
SOLOMON

• Hamath

• Kadesh

PHOENICIA

• Damascus

Sidon •

Tyre •   • Dan   SYRIA

THE GREAT SEA   GESHUR
(Mediterranean)

GILEAD

Megiddo •

River Jordan

ISRAEL

Bethel •
Gibeon •   • Gibeah   AMMON
Jerusalem •

Gath
Gaza •   Hebron •   ARABIAN DESERT
PHILISTIA

JUDAH   Dead Sea

Beersheba •   MOAB

EGYPT
River of

AMALEKITES   EDOM

ARABAH DESERT

EGYPT

0   20   50

Scale of Miles

Ezion-geber •
Gulf of Aqaba

army, was able to restore enough order to have Ishbosheth (Eshbaal) anointed as king in Gilead east of the Jordan. Philistine interference or occupation may have delayed the accession of Saul's son for five years, since he ruled only two years during the seven and a half years that David reigned at Hebron.

David was in Philistia when news reached him of Saul's death. After mourning the deaths of Saul and Jonathan, David returned to Hebron where he was anointed as king by the leaders of Judah. Although civil strife prevailed in Israel with the tribe of Judah supporting David and the rest of the nation loyal to Ishbosheth, mediation was soon effected when all Israel realized that David held no animosity toward the family of Saul. In the course of these negotiations, both Abner and Ishbosheth were slain without the consent of David. After seven and a half years David gained recognition of all the tribes of Israel without malice or vengeance.

	II Samuel	I Chronicles
I. The Conquest of Jerusalem	5:1-9	11:1-9
II. David's Military Strength	23:8-39	11:10—12:40
III. Recognition by Philistia and Phoenicia	5:10-25	14:1-17
IV. Jerusalem—Center of Religion	6:1-23	13:1-14
		15:1—16:43
V. An Eternal Throne	7:1-29	17:1-27

JERUSALEM—THE NATIONAL CAPITAL David's kingship at Hebron may have been no serious concern of the Philistines, but when David won the acclaim and recognition of the entire nation of Israel the Philistines were seriously alarmed. Twice David defeated them and may have found their opposition an aid to the unification of Israel.

Jerusalem had remained a Jebusite stronghold throughout the time that Israel had occupied Canaan. After David decided that this would be a strategic location for a national capital, Joab succeeded in expelling the Jebusites and as a reward became commander of David's army. The particular site which David occupied was known as Ophel and may have been higher at that time than the hill to the north where the temple was built under Solomon. This fortress was known as the "city of David" (I Chron. 11:7) and was frequently referred to as Zion in subsequent Old Testament literature because it represented the seat of authority in Israel.

When David assumed national leadership, he organized the entire nation. The men who had been with him as a fugitive and at Hebron were now appointed as princes and leaders. He built a magnificent palace in Jerusalem, contracting with the Phoenicians for his material (II Sam. 5:11, 12).

Jerusalem was also made the religious center of Israel. In time, the ark was brought to Jerusalem and housed in a tent or tabernacle. Priests and Levites were assigned their respective duties, and worship was reestablished on a national scale.

David was vitally interested in building a temple. Although Nathan the prophet at first approved, he was subsequently divinely instructed that the building of the temple would be postponed until David's son was established on the throne. This was because David was essentially a man of war, and though he was a man after God's own heart, David's son Solomon would build the temple. The magnitude of the promise made to David, however, extends far beyond the scope and time of Solomon's kingdom. David was assured that his throne would be established forever. Sin and iniquity in David's posterity would be temporarily judged and punished, but God promised not to withdraw His mercy indefinitely.

No earthly kingdom or dynasty has ever had eternal duration. Neither did the earthly throne of David—without linking his lineage to Jesus, who is specifically identified in the New Testament as the Son of David. This assurance, given to David through the prophet Nathan, constitutes another link in the series of Messianic promises given in Old Testament times. A fuller revelation of the Messiah and His eternal kingdom is given by the prophets in subsequent centuries.

	II Samuel	I Chronicles
I. List of Nations Conquered	8:1-13	18:1-13
II. David Shares Responsibility and Blessing	8:15—9:13	18:14-17
III. The Famine	21:1-14	
IV. Defeat of Ammonites, Syrians, and Philistines	10:1-18 21:15-22	19:1—20:8
V. Song of Deliverance (Ps. 18)	22:1-51	

PROSPERITY AND SUPREMACY The expansion of Davidic rule from the tribal boundaries of Judah to a vast empire stretching its domain from the River of Egypt and the Gulf of Aqaba to regions of the Euphrates receives scant attention in the Biblical record. Historically, however, this is very significant since the Davidic and Solomonic kingdom of Israel was the leading nation in the Fertile Crescent at the beginning of the tenth century B.C.

The observations that the Philistines had the monopoly on iron in the days of Samuel (I Sam. 13:19, 20), and that near the end of David's reign it was freely used in Israel (I Chron. 22:3), suggest that a long chapter could have been written on the economic revolution in Israel. David's period as a fugitive and Philistine residence not only afforded him experience in military leadership, but also gave him firsthand acquaintance with the formula and methods used by the Philistines in the production of arms.

The Arabah Desert, which extended southward from the Dead Sea to the Gulf of Aqaba, was strategically important for Israel. The iron and copper deposits in this area were necessary to break the Philistine monopoly. In all likelihood this was the reason that David conquered and occupied Edom and established garrisons throughout the land to control these natural resources (II Sam. 8:14).

In addition to defeating the Philistines and the Edomites, David subdued the Moabites and Amalekites, exacting silver and gold from them. David also defeated the Ammonites and Arameans, extending his power east and north to gain control of the trade routes that came through Damascus and other points. With the Phoenicians who carried on lucrative naval trade, David concluded a treaty.

The story of Mephibosheth given in the narratives of Israel's expansion illustrates David's magnanimous attitude toward his predecessor's descendants. David not only allotted Mephibosheth a pension from the royal treasury, but also provided a home for him in Jerusalem.

Mephibosheth received special consideration during a famine that came as a judgment upon Israel for Saul's terrible crime of attempting to exterminate the Gibeonites with whom Joshua had made a covenant (cf. Josh. 9:3, ff.). Realizing that this sin required atonement (Num. 35:31, ff.), David allowed the Gibeonites to execute seven of Saul's descendants. Mephibosheth, however, was spared. At this time David transferred the bones of Saul and Jonathan to the family sepulcher in Benjamin.

As king of Israel, David did not fail to acknowledge God as the One who granted Israel military victories and material prosperity. In a psalm of thanksgiving (II Sam. 22; Ps. 18), David expressed his praise. This represents but a sample of many psalms that he composed on various occasions during his varied career as a shepherd boy, a servant in the royal court, a fugitive of Israel, and finally as the architect-king and builder of Israel's largest empire.

SIN IN THE Character imperfections in the leaders of Israel are
ROYAL FAMILY[1] not minimized in the Bible. Indulging in sin, David
could not escape the judgments of God, but when he
acknowledged his iniquity as a penitent sinner he qualified as a man who pleased God (I Sam. 13:14).

I. David's Crime and Repentance	II Samuel 11:1—12:31
II. Amnon's Crime and Results	13:1-36
III. Absalom's Defeat in Rebellion	13:37—18:33
IV. David Recovers the Throne	19:1—20:26

---

[1] This account is exclusively recorded in II Samuel.

David practiced polygamy (II Sam. 3:2-5; 11:27). In Davidic times a harem at the royal court was a status symbol and freely practiced by surrounding nations. Polygamy seems to have been tolerated in Old Testament times because of the hardness of Israel's heart, but was definitely forbidden in the fuller revelation of the New Testament. Kings were especially warned about the multiplicity of wives (Deut. 17:17). For David, the marriages to Michal the daughter of Saul and Maacah the daughter of Talmai, king of Geshur, had political implications. Like others, David had to suffer the consequences as the crimes of incest, murder, and rebellion unfolded in his family life.

From the human standpoint, David's sin of adultery with Bathsheba and the murder of Uriah constituted a perfect crime. Not accountable to anyone in his kingdom, David very likely concealed these developments from everyone but temporarily failed to recognize that his thoughts and deeds were known to God. For a despot in a heathen nation, adultery and murder might have passed unchallenged, but not so in Israel where kingship was a sacred trust. When confronted with his sin by Nathan the prophet, David repented. David's spiritual crises found lofty expressions in Psalms 32 and 51. He was granted forgiveness but grave, indeed, were the domestic consequences (II Sam. 12:11). The grace of God is seen in the fact that God spared David from death by stoning which was the scriptural punishment for adultery. It is further seen in that David's illegitimate child was overshadowed by Bathsheba's giving birth to Solomon who later became king.

David's lack of discipline and self-restraint set a poor example for his sons who became involved in immorality and murder. Amnon's immoral behavior with his half sister resulted in his assassination by Absalom. Incurring David's disfavor, Absalom found refuge with Talmai, his grandfather in Geshur, for three years but then returned to Jerusalem through Joab's mediation. After spending about four years in Jerusalem in a public relations effort to win the hearts of the people, Absalom staged a rebellion against David which appeared to have all the marks of success when David was taken by surprise and forced to flee from Jerusalem.

David was a brilliant militarist. Given time to organize his forces, David routed the armies of his rebellious son. Absalom was killed. David, who mourned his son's death instead of celebrating the victory, was rebuked by Joab for neglecting the welfare of the Israelites who had given him loyal support. After another rebellion led by Sheba, a Benjaminite, was suppressed, David recovered his throne.

Through nearly a decade following David's crime, the solemn words spoken by Nathan the prophet were realistically fulfilled. God indeed had forgiven and pardoned David's sin, but he had to suffer the consequences that fermented in his own house.

	II Samuel	I Chronicles
I. Sin in Numbering the People	24:1-25	21:1-27
II. Solomon Charged to Build the Temple		21:28—22:19
III. Duties of Levites		23:1—26:28
IV. Civil Officers		26:29—27:34
V. Charge to Officials and People		28:1—29:22
VI. Last Words of David	23:1-7	
VII. Death of David		29:22-30

RETROSPECT David made elaborate plans and detailed arrangements
AND PROSPECT for building the temple. Although he had defeated
surrounding nations in his expansion of the Israelite
empire, David had made a treaty with the Phoenicians who carried on
extensive naval commerce throughout the Mediterranean world. With the
Phoenicians, David negotiated for the materials to build the temple. Local
and foreign labor was organized for this purpose and even the details
for religious worship in the proposed structure were carefully outlined.

The military census of Israel and the punitive consequences for the
king and his people were closely related to David's elaborate plans for
building the temple. Even though the reason for divine punishment upon
the king and his people is not clearly stated, it seems as though David
was motivated by pride and reliance on military strength for Israel's
national achievements. Perhaps Israel was punished for the rebellions
under Absalom and Sheba. Although Joab objected to taking the census,
David overruled.

Punishment for this sin was announced by Gad the prophet. Given the
choice of punishment, David resigned himself and his nation to God's
mercy by choosing the pestilence. During these days of judgment, David
and the elders offered intercessory prayer on the threshing floor of
Ornan, the Jebusite, directly north of Jerusalem. Instructed by Gad,
David purchased this site. As he offered a sacrifice there before God,
he became conscious of a divine response as the pestilence ceased.

This site, Mount Moriah, was designated by David as the location for
the altar of burnt offering and the temple. Very likely this was the spot
where Abraham, approximately a millennium earlier, had been willing
to offer his son Isaac. Although Mount Moriah was outside the city of
Zion (Jerusalem) as originally occupied by David, it was included in
the capital city under Solomon.

David reflected on the fact that he had been a man of war and bloodshed. The first seven and a half years at Hebron had been a period of
preparation and civil strife. During the next decade, Jerusalem was
established as the national capital and many surrounding nations were
defeated in the expansion of the kingdom. David's sin and the subsequent
rebellions may have disrupted the major part of the third decade of

his reign. During the last decade David focused his attention upon the preparation for building the temple that he was not permitted to erect. David charged Solomon with the responsibility to obey the Law as it had been given to Moses and to acknowledge his accountability to God. In a public assembly, David charged the princes and priesthood to recognize Solomon as his successor.

The last words of David (II Sam. 23:1-7) reveal the greatness of Israel's most honored hero. He speaks prophetically about the eternal endurance of his kingdom. God had spoken to him, affirming an everlasting covenant. This testimony by David would have made a fitting epitaph for his tomb.

Guide Questions for Study and Discussion

1. What part of David's reign is exclusively recorded in II Samuel?
2. Who were the army captains under Saul and David?
3. How did David show his kindness to the family of Saul?
4. Why was David denied the privilege of building the temple?
5. Name two prophets in the reign of David.
6. What economic resources did David secure from the Sinaitic area?
7. How did David's exile in Philistia prepare him for the future?
8. Why was Absalom ostracized from Jerusalem?
9. Who misguided Absalom in his strategy?
10. Whom did David designate as his successor?

Activities for Enrichment and Application

1. Compare and contrast content and approach to history found in the books of II Samuel and I Chronicles. What is the place of God in current historical events?
2. List the nations conquered by David and show on a map how his kingdom expanded. How does this compare with the borders of the land God gave as inheritance to Israel (Gen. 15:18)? What spiritual application can be made from this study?
3. Trace the consequences of David's sin during his reign. What aspects of God's manner of judgment for sin have not altered since David's time? Give Biblical verification for your answer.
4. Compare and contrast the characters of Saul and David. What characteristics in their lives exemplify characteristics of leaders you know personally?
5. What traits of David's kingship foreshadow Israel's greater King, Christ?

Significant Resources

EDERSHEIM, ALFRED. *Old Testament Bible History*. Grand Rapids: Wm. B. Eerdmans Pub. Co., 1972.

FREE, JOSEPH P. *Archaeology and Bible History*. Wheaton, IL: Scripture Press, 1976.

JONES, T. H. "David" in *The New Bible Dictionary*. Ed. by J. D. Douglas. Grand Rapids: Wm. B. Eerdmans Pub. Co., 1962.

UNGER, MERRILL F. *Archaeology and the Old Testament*. Grand Rapids: Zondervan Pub. House, 1954.

WRIGHT, GEORGE E. *Biblical Archaeology*. Philadelphia: Westminster Press, 1963.

CHAPTER EIGHT

The Solomonic Kingdom

SCRIPTURE SURVEY: I Kings 1—11; II Chronicles 1—9

EXTENT OF TIME: ca. 971-931 B.C.

Peace and prosperity—these two words describe the golden era of Solomon's reign over Israel. He reaped the benefits of his father's military efforts in uniting the nation, expanding the borders of Israel, and gaining international recognition.

Solomon's reign of forty years as given in these two accounts is difficult to outline in any chronological order. The building and dedication of the temple which occurred during the first decade receive the most consideration in these records. The building of the palace was completed thirteen years later. Many activities which are barely mentioned have been illuminated in recent years through archaeological excavations. Lacking a chronological perspective, the Biblical content is considered topically in this analysis of the accounts in I Kings and II Chronicles.

	I Kings	II Chronicles
I. Solomon Emerges as Sole Ruler	1:1—2:46	
II. Prayer for Wisdom at Gibeon	3:1-15	1:1-13
III. Wisdom in Administration	3:16—4:34	
IV. Trade and Prosperity		1:14-17

SOLOMON ESTABLISHED AS KING Solomon inherited the throne of his father David. Although Adonijah, another son of David, enlisted the support of Joab and Abiathar, the priest at Jerusalem, to have himself anointed as king, the appeal of the prophet Nathan and Solomon's mother Bathsheba to David resulted in recognizing Solomon as king. He was anointed on the eastern slope of Mount Ophel by Zadok, the officiating priest at Gibeah. In a public acclaim, "Long live King Solomon!", the people of Jerusalem expressed their support so effectively that the supporters of Adonijah dispersed.

In a subsequent convocation, Solomon was officially crowned and recognized by the nation (I Chron. 28:1). With officials and statesmen representing the whole nation present, David delivered a charge to the people outlining their responsibilities to Solomon, the king of God's choice. Privately, David reminded his son that he was responsible to obey the Law of Moses (I Kings 2:1-12).

Numerous changes occurred as Solomon was established on the throne. Adonijah's request to marry Abishag, the Shunamite maiden, was interpreted by Solomon as treason resulting in Adonijah's execution. The removal and banishment of Abiathar to Anathoth marked the fulfillment of the solemn words spoken to Eli (cf. I Sam. 2:27-36; I Kings 2:26, 27). Joab's treasonable conduct in supporting Adonijah and his crimes during David's reign brought about his execution.

As a young man possibly in his early twenties, Solomon sensed his need for wisdom as he assumed national leadership. Sacrificing at Gibeon where the tabernacle and the bronze altar were located, he received the divine assurance that his request for wisdom would be granted. Conditioned on his obedience, he was also assured of riches, honor, and long life.

Solomon's wisdom as king of Israel became a source of wonderment. The wise judgment rendered by Solomon in the case recorded in I Kings 3:16-28 very likely represents but a sample of many decisions that exhibited his wisdom before his people. Internationally, his fame spread through extensive trade (II Chron. 1:14-17).

Solomon's kingdom may have been very simple at the beginning but became a vast organization in the course of controlling his vast empire. The king himself constituted the final court of appeals. Appointments of various officers are listed in I Kings 4:1-6 and represent an increase over those under David. For taxation purposes the nation was divided into twelve districts. In rotation, each district supplied provisions for the central government during one month of each year from a store city or from warehouses where these supplies were collected during the rest of the year. One day's supply for the king and his court of army and building personnel consisted of over 300 bushels of flour, almost 700 bushels of meal, 10 fattened cattle, 20 pasture-fed cattle, 100 sheep, plus other animals and fowl (I Kings 4:22-23). Solomon also added to his armed forces 1,400 chariots and 12,000 horsemen which were stationed in Jerusalem and chariot cities throughout Israel. This added to the burden of taxation a regular supply of barley and hay. Through efficient organization and wise administration, Israel maintained a state of prosperity and progress.

THE BUILDING PROGRAM   The temple constructed by Solomon represented a high point in Israel's religious history. It marked the fulfillment of David's desire to establish a permanent place of worship. The significant events include:

	I Kings	II Chronicles
I. The Temple in Jerusalem	5:1—7:51	2:1—5:1
II. Solomon's Palace	7:1-8	

III. Dedication of the Temple   8:1—9:9   5:2—8:16
IV. Settlement with Hiram of Tyre   9:10-25

Through treaty arrangements with Hiram, the wealthy and powerful ruler of Tyre and Sidon who had extensive commercial contacts throughout the Mediterranean world, vast resources were available to Solomon. Advanced in architecture and workmanship of costly building materials, the Phoenicians not only furnished building supplies, but also thousands of architects, technicians, and foremen who supervised building the temple in Jerusalem. Solomon made payment in grain, oil, and wine.

The temple was erected on the top of Mount Moriah located directly north of Zion where David had built his palace. On this place, where Abraham had gone to sacrifice Isaac, Solomon's temple stood until it was destroyed in 586 B.C. by Nebuchadnezzar. It was rebuilt in 520-515 B.C. and demolished in A.D. 70. Since the seventh century A.D. the Mohammedan mosque, the Dome of the Rock, has been located on this site which is regarded as the most sacred spot in world history. Today this temple area very likely is larger than it was in Solomon's time, covering about thirty-five to forty acres.

The temple itself was twice as large as the Mosaic tabernacle in its basic floor area. As a permanent structure it was much more elaborate and spacious, with appropriate additions and a much larger surrounding court. Although no archaeological remains are known to modern excavators, it is quite likely that the art and architecture were basically Phoenician. Descriptions indicate that the temple and its furnishings were very elaborate with gold being used freely. The splendor and beauty of this temple apparently were never equaled in the history of Israel.[1]

DEDICATION
OF THE TEMPLE
The dedication of the temple was the most significant event in the religious history of the nation since Israel left Mount Sinai. Not without importance is the chronological notation in I Kings 6:1 relating the deliverance of Israel from Egypt and the building of the temple. Whereas the pillar of cloud hovered over the tabernacle, the glory of God was manifested in the dedication of the temple signifying God's blessing and benediction. The temple was dedicated as the Israelites gathered in Jerusalem to observe the Feast of Tabernacles which also reminded them that they once were pilgrims in the wilderness. With Solomon as king, the kingdom of Israel was divinely confirmed as anticipated by Moses (Deut. 17:14-20).

Solomon was the key person in the dedication ceremonies. Under the covenant all Israelites were God's servants (Lev. 25:42, 55; Jer. 30:10,

---

[1] For a fuller description of the temple and its furnishings, see Schultz, *The Old Testament Speaks*, pp. 144-147.

and other passages) and viewed as a kingdom of priests unto God (Ex. 19:6). Solomon, in his unique position as king of God's chosen people, took the position of a servant of God in representing his nation in the dedication ceremonies. This relationship with God was common to prophet, priest, layman, and king in true recognition of the dignity of man. In this capacity Solomon offered prayer, delivered the dedicatory address, and officiated at the offering of sacrifice.

Solomon also built an elaborate palace for himself which took thirteen years to complete. It contained government offices, living quarters for the daughter of Pharaoh, and his own private residence. In addition, the maintenance of the powerful army and the administration of the kingdom required building numerous cities such as Megiddo throughout the land.

INTERNATIONAL   David had already taken control of Edom and the
RELATIONS   vast natural resources extending south to the Gulf of
                              Aqaba. Recent archaeological findings [2] indicate that
Ezion-geber was a large refining center of iron and copper in the days of Solomon. Aided by Phoenician engineers, the city became the "Pittsburgh of Palestine."

	I Kings	II Chronicles
I. Naval Ventures at Ezion-geber	9:26-28	8:17, 18
II. The Queen of Sheba	10:1-13	9:1-12
III. Revenue and Trade	10:14-29	9:13-31

Control of this metal industry placed the Israelites in an advantageous position in commerce and trade. Through the aid of the Phoenicians, Solomon built ships that took iron and copper as far as southwest Arabia (modern Yemen) and the African coast of Ethiopia from where they returned with gold, silver, ivory, and monkeys. Phoenician commerce provided favorable contacts with the Mediterranean world. As a result, Solomon accumulated extensive wealth.

Horses and chariots were acquired by Solomon from the Hittites through the Arameans. Although David hamstrung or lamed all the horses he captured, with the exception of one hundred (II Sam. 8:4), it is obvious that Solomon accumulated a considerable force. These were helpful for controlling the commerce that crossed Israel's territory. Additional wealth was accrued to Israel by establishing vast camel caravans to promote spice trade between Southern Arabia, Syria, Phoenicia, and Egypt.

International respect and recognition increased Solomon's wealth by gifts from rulers far and near. People from afar came to hear the wisdom

---

[2] Nelson Glueck, *The Other Side of the Jordan* (New Haven, Yale Sta.: Am. Schools of Oriental Research, 1940), p. 94.

of this Hebrew king expressed in his proverbs, songs, and speeches. The visit of the Queen of Sheba may represent but a sample of the international acclaim. Her 1,200 mile trip by camel very likely was motivated by commercial interests. The wealth and wisdom of Solomon was never exceeded by any Israelite king.

APOSTASY AND DEATH   Tragic and disappointing is the final chapter of Solomon's reign as reported in I Kings chapter eleven. The simple facts are that the king who had reached the zenith of success and fame in wisdom, wealth, and international acclaim under the divine blessing terminated his reign in failure. Like the Israelites in the wilderness after God's revelation to them at Mount Sinai, Solomon departed from wholehearted devotion to God. He broke the very first commandment by his inclusive policy of allowing idol worship at Jerusalem.

A. Foreign wives and idolatry

Solomon also conformed to contemporary culture by making alliances with foreign rulers and confirming this by marriage (I Kings 11:1-8). By taking wives from Egypt, the Moabites, Ammonites, Edomites, Sidonians, and Hittites, Solomon permitted idolatry to prevail in the environs of the temple he had erected unto God. The multiplicity of wives resulted in his ruination, as his heart was turned away from God (Deut. 17:17). Some of the gods which Solomon recognized by building high places for them were not removed until the times of Josiah, three and a half centuries later (II Kings 23:13).

B. Judgment and adversaries

While Solomon was still living, the stage was set for the disruption of the kingdom. Because of disobedience, the kingdom was to be divided according to the words of the prophet Ahijah (I Kings 11:9-43). For David's sake, the judgment was withheld until after the death of Solomon. Enemies and strong leaders such as Hadad the Edomite, Rezon of Damascus, and Jeroboam, to whom the prophet Ahijah gave ten pieces of his mantle to indicate that he would rule over ten tribes, began to threaten the rule of Solomon. Even though the kingdom was sustained and not divided until after his death, Solomon was subjected to the anguish of rebellion at home and secession in various parts of his empire as a result of his personal failure to obey and serve God faithfully.

Guide Questions for Study and Discussion

1. What was Solomon's greatest concern when he became king?
2 Who furnished architects, foremen, and building supplies for the temple?

3. Describe briefly the temple itself.
4. How did Solomon make payment for the building material?
5. Describe briefly the dedication of the temple.
6. How was God's presence apparent at the dedication?
7. Why did the Queen of Sheba come to see Solomon?
8. What physical factors aided Solomon in accumulating great wealth?
9. How did foreign wives influence Solomon?
10. Why did God withhold judgment upon Solomon during his life?

Activities for Enrichment and Application

1. What characteristics and abilities made Solomon a great king and leader? What characteristics and weaknesses led to his decline? Which of these are applicable to Christian leadership?
2. Compare and contrast the reign of Solomon with the reign of his father David. What factors of parental influence can be observed in this study?
3. Trace the events leading to the division of the kingdom. What specific sin was the root of the problems? Discuss the extent of its consequence.
4. What great principles of prayer worthy of emulation can be observed in Solomon's dedicatory prayer?
5. Compare the dedication of the temple with the dedication of the tabernacle. What aspects of these dedications could be applied in the dedication of a new church building?

Significant Resources

CROCKETT, WILLIAM DAY. A Harmony of Samuel, Kings, and Chronicles. Grand Rapids: Baker Book House, 1951.
FINEGAN, JACK. Light from the Ancient Past: The Archaeological Background of Judaism and Christianity. 2nd ed. Princeton, NJ: Princeton Univ. Press, 1959.
FREE, JOSEPH P. Archaeology and Bible History. Wheaton, IL: Scripture Press, 1976.
HUBBARD, D. A. "Solomon" in The New Bible Dictionary. Ed. by J. D. Douglas. Grand Rapids: Wm. B. Eerdmans Pub. Co., 1962.

CHAPTER NINE

The Northern Kingdom

SCRIPTURE SURVEY: I Kings 12—22; II Kings 1—17
EXTENT OF TIME: ca. 931-722 B.C.

Rebellion after the death of Solomon resulted in the division of the Davidic empire. To the north, ten tribes rebelled against the Davidic dynasty ruling in Jerusalem and established the Northern Kingdom under the leadership of Jeroboam. Beyond the Northern Kingdom to the northeast, the Syrians or Arameans declared their independence under the leadership of Rezon with Damascus as their capital. Rehoboam the son of Solomon retained only the tribes of Judah and Benjamin for his kingdom, continuing to use Jerusalem as his capital.

The biblical account of the Northern Kingdom is given in I Kings 12 to II Kings 17. Interwoven with it are the contemporary events in the Southern Kingdom. Although the name Israel was originally given to Jacob and subsequently used to designate his descendants, it was normally used during the divided kingdom era to refer to the Northern Kingdom.[1]

The Northern Kingdom lasted approximately two centuries (931-722 B.C.). Changes in ruling families or dynasties occurred quite frequently. For our study purposes the developments in the Northern Kingdom may be conveniently divided as given below. Of special interest also are the prophets who ministered during these centuries confronting the kings and the people with God's message.

I. Dynasty of Jeroboam, 931-909 B.C.	I Kings 12—15
II. Dynasty of Baasha, 909-885 B.C.	I Kings 15—16
III. Dynasty of Omri, 885-841 B.C.	I Kings 16—22; II Kings 1—9
IV. Dynasty of Jehu, 841-752 B.C.	II Kings 10—15
V. Last Kings of Israel, 752-722 B.C.	II Kings 15—17

THE ROYAL FAMILY OF JEROBOAM Jeroboam distinguished himself as an efficient administrator under Solomon who placed him in charge of constructing the wall of Jerusalem, known as Millo. A prophet named Ahijah dramatically conveyed to Jeroboam the future developments by giving him ten pieces of his mantle

---

[1] The name "Ephraim" which originally referred to Joseph's son and later to one of the tribes is also used to designate the Northern Kingdom (cf. Isa. 7; Hosea).

signifying that Jeroboam would rule over ten tribes (I Kings 11). Arousing the suspicion of Solomon, Jeroboam temporarily took refuge in Egypt but returned to Shechem when the elders of Israel rebelled against Rehoboam. Here he was recognized as the first king of the Northern Kingdom, reigning for twenty-two years. Although civil warfare and bloodshed were averted at this time of secession, periodic wars between Jeroboam and Rehoboam erupted which are merely noted in the biblical record (II Chron. 12:15).

A. Religious trends

In religious matters Jeroboam took the initiative in leading his people astray. Fearing that his people might be diverted in their political loyalty by going to Jerusalem to worship, Jeroboam instituted idolatry by erecting golden calves at Bethel and Dan. Ignoring Mosaic restrictions, he appointed priests and allowed the Israelites to offer sacrifices at high places throughout the land. Jeroboam even officiated at the altar and changed feast days (cf. I Kings 12:25-33).

B. Warned by two prophets

The experience of an unnamed prophet from Judah is dramatically portrayed in I Kings 13. Jeroboam is realistically confronted with a warning that tempered his aggressiveness in promoting idolatry. The sequel to the faithful ministry of this unnamed prophet deserves careful study. Perhaps the tomb of this prophet, who was killed by a lion and brought back to Bethel for burial, serves as a reminder to succeeding generations that obedience to God is essential even for a messenger of God.

Another prophet who warned Jeroboam was Ahijah. When Jeroboam's wife inquired of Ahijah regarding the prospect of the recovery of their son Abijah, the king of Israel was not only informed that his son would die but that the dynasty of Jeroboam would be exterminated. This was divine judgment for failure to obey the commandments of God.

When Jeroboam died, his son Nadab ruled only two years. He was assassinated by Baasha.

THE DYNASTY OF BAASHA Little is known about Baasha, of the tribe of Issachar, who became the next king of Israel. Apparently he made Tirzah the capital. When many of his people seemed to desert to Judah, Baasha began to fortify the city of Ramah where the two main roads from the north converge, leading to Jerusalem only five miles south. Fearing these developments, King Asa of Jerusalem bribed Benhadad of Damascus to attack Israel. When Benhadad took control of such cities as Kedesh, Hazor, Merom, and Zephath, and acquired the rich fertile acreage west of Lake Galilee, the Syrians accrued the lucrative returns from the caravan trade to the Phoenician coast. As a result, Baasha abandoned his fortification of Ramah, averting war with Judah.

A. The prophet Jehu

Jehu, the son of Hanani, was active in proclaiming God's message during the reign of Baasha. He reminded the king that he should serve God who had entrusted him with the kingship, but unfortunately Baasha continued in the sinful idolatrous ways of Jeroboam.

B. Elah the king

Elah, the son of Baasha, ruled less than two years. While in a state of drunkenness, Elah was assassinated by Zimri. The prophetic words of Jehu were fulfilled as Zimri exterminated the friends and relatives of this ruling family. Zimri, however, ruled only seven days.

THE ROYAL FAMILY OF OMRI The most notorious dynasty in the Northern Kingdom was established by Omri. Best known in this family was his son Ahab who was succeeded by his two sons, Ahaziah and Joram. During this period Israel not only regained much territory lost in Syria, but also gained international renown.

A. Omri the king

When Zimri slew Elah, the Israelite troops—encamped against Gibbethon—were under Omri's command. When Omri marched his troops against Tirzah, Zimri secluded himself in the palace while it was reduced to ashes. When Tibni who apparently was a strong leader died six years later, Omri was sole ruler of Israel.

Omri's twelve-year reign is summarized in eight verses in the Bible (I Kings 16:21-28). His reign, however, was very significant. He built the city of Samaria on a site seven miles northwest of Shechem. Strategically located on the road leading to Phoenicia, Galilee, and Esdraelon, Samaria was secured as the impregnable capital of Israel for over a century and a half until it was conquered by the Assyrians in 722 B.C.

Omri promoted an international policy that established Israel's prestige. Apparently he subjected the Moabites, exacting taxes from them. He made an alliance with Phoenicia which was sealed by the marriage of his son Ahab to Jezebel, the daughter of Ethbaal the king of the Sidonians. This relationship was commercially advantageous to Israel, but resulted in a degrading religious fusion in the next generation. Very likely Omri regained the economic and territorial losses Baasha had suffered under Syrian aggression. So great and extensive was Omri's international fame that in subsequent times the Assyrian records referred to Israel as the land of Omri.

B. Ahab and Jezebel

Ahab, the son of Omri, expanded the political and commercial interests of Israel during his twenty-two-year reign. Increasing trade with the Phoenicians represented a serious threat to the lucrative trading interests of Syria. A policy of friendship with Judah, sealed by the marriage of Ahab's daughter Athaliah to Jehoram the son of Jehoshaphat, strengthened Israel against Syria. From Moab, Ahab exacted a heavy tribute of livestock. With wealth accruing to Israel through these economic policies, Ahab was able to build and fortify many cities including Jericho, and to lavish wealth on himself by building an "ivory house" (I Kings 22:39).

C. Ahab's religion

Baal worship was promoted under Ahab and Jezebel. To this god of Tyre, the king of Israel built a temple in the city of Samaria and, by bringing hundreds of prophets into Israel, Baalism became the religion of Ahab's people. Consequently, Ahab gained the reputation of being the most sinful of all the kings who ruled Israel. Notoriously, Jezebel is portrayed as the degrading influence behind the throne.

D. Elijah the prophet

Elijah stepped forth in this era of rank apostasy as a forthright spokesman for God. After a three-and-a-half year drought, he dramatically challenged Baalism and supervised the execution of Jezebel's prophets on Mount Carmel. Fearing the queen, Elijah retreated to the Sinai Peninsula where he received a threefold commission: to anoint Hazael as king of Syria, to anoint Jehu as king of Israel, and to call Elisha as his successor. On his return to Israel, Elijah called Elisha to be his associate in the prophetic ministry.

A final encounter between Elijah and Ahab took place in Naboth's vineyard (I Kings 21:1-29). Ruthless Jezebel, who had no respect for Israelite law and gave no heed to Naboth's conscientious refusal to sell his inherited possession to the king, engineered the stoning of Naboth. As Ahab took possession of this vineyard, he was severely rebuked by Elijah. For this gross injustice in shedding innocent blood, the Omride dynasty was doomed. Ahab's repentance tempered this judgment only by postponement until after his death.

E. Warfare with Syria

Toward the end of Ahab's reign there seemed to have been frequent warfare with Syria. When faced by a common enemy, however, Israel and Syria joined forces as is indicated by the battle of Karkar. Shortly after this, Ahab persuaded Jehoshaphat the king of Judah to join him in a battle against Syria (I Kings 22:1-40). After Ahab was warned by the prophet Micaiah that he would be killed in this battle, Ahab disguised himself so that he would not be recognized by the Syrians. However, a stray arrow pierced Ahab, wounding him fatally and fulfilling the words of Elijah (I Kings 21:19).

F. Ahaziah, king of Israel

This son of Ahab ruled only one year. He failed to suppress the rebellion of Moab and unsuccessfully launched naval expeditions with Jehoshaphat at the Gulf of Aqaba. Elijah's last encounter with the Omride dynasty in the biblical account was the warning to Ahaziah that he would not recover (II Kings 1).

G. Joram, the son of Ahab

The twelve-year reign of Joram terminated the Omride rule in Israel in 841 B.C. During these years, intermittent warfare was carried on between Israel and Syria. Apparently Syria increased in military strength so that when Joram's reign ended, Syria emerged as the dominating kingdom in Palestine.

ELIJAH AND ELISHA   These two prophets had cooperated in establishing schools for prophets throughout Israel. Apparently Elijah's ascension occurred near the beginning of Joram's reign so that Elisha became the leading prophet in Israel. Numerous events are recorded in which Elisha was closely associated with Joram in his military problems as he sought to regain control of Moab and fight against Syria.

Elisha's ministry was known not only throughout Israel but also in Syria as well as in Judah and Edom. Through the healing of Naaman and the peculiar encounter of the Syrian armies with this prophet, Elisha was recognized as the "man of God" even in the Syrian capital Damascus. Near the end of Joram's reign, Elisha made a visit to Damascus to inform Hazael that he would be the next king of Syria (II Kings 8:7-15). While Joram was recovering at Jezreel from a wound he had received in battle, Elisha sent his servant to anoint Jehu king of Israel. Being commander of the Israelite army, Jehu proclaimed himself king and killed Joram the king of Israel as well as Ahaziah the king of Judah.

THE DYNASTY   This ruling family occupied the throne of the Northern
OF JEHU   Kingdom for a longer period than any other dynasty—
                    nearly a century (841-753 B.C.). During this time

Israel rose from an extremely weakened position to a strong kingdom reaching its peak in international prestige and prosperity under Jeroboam II.

A. Jehu

A bloody revolution brought Jehu to the throne. Not only did Jehu dispose of the royal family including Jezebel, but he also exterminated Baalism, making a clean sweep in religion and politics. By exterminating the Omride family, Jehu incurred the disfavor of Phoenicia and Judah. Seeking to avert Assyrian aggression, he sent tribute to Shalmaneser III but thereby faced the antagonism of Hazael, king of Syria, who enlarged his kingdom southward by claiming Gilead and Bashan at Israel's expense. Idolatry however prevailed under Jehu.

B. Jehoahaz

When Jehu died in 814 B.C., Hazael took further advantage of Israel during the reign of Jehoahaz. So weak was Israel at this time that Hazael advanced his armies through Israel to capture Gath and threaten Jerusalem (II Kings 12:17). Jehoahaz was so helpless that he was ineffective in resisting invasion by the Edomites, Ammonites, Philistines, and Tyrians. Although Jehoahaz temporarily turned to God for relief from this pressure, he did not depart from idolatry nor destroy the images of the gods in Samaria (II Kings 13:1-9).

C. Jehoash

During the reign of Jehoash (798-782 B.C.), Israel's successes revived. With the death of Hazael (ca. 800 B.C.), the Syrian power declined. Israel built up a strong fighting force, placing Benhadad II of Syria on the defensive, and reclaimed much territory. When Jehoash was challenged by Amaziah of Judah, the Israelite army invaded Judah, broke down part of the wall of Jerusalem, plundered the palace and temple, and even took hostages back to Samaria.

Elisha the prophet was still living when Jehoash began to reign. The silence of the Scriptures warrants the conclusion that neither Jehu nor Jehoahaz had much to do with Elisha, but Jehoash went down to see Elisha on his deathbed. In a dramatic incident the prophet assured victory over Syria to the king of Israel. Although Jehoash was disturbed over the loss of Elisha, he did not serve God nor turn from his idolatrous ways. His reign, however, marked the turning point in the blessings of Israel as Elisha had predicted.

D. King Jeroboam II

Jeroboam, the fourth ruler in Jehu's dynasty, was the outstanding king in the Northern Kingdom, ruling forty-one years including a twelve-year coregency with his father (793-753 B.C.). The vast political and commercial expansion of Israel under his leadership is summarized in the prophecy given by Jonah (II Kings 14:23-29). With Syria being threatened by Assyria, it was possible for Jeroboam to regain Israelite borders to the east and north. The wall of Samaria was widened and the city refortified. Peace and prosperity unequaled since the days of Solomon brought to Israel wealth and luxury reflected in the books of Amos and Hosea. With it came the moral decline and religious indifference which these two prophets boldly challenged.

When Jeroboam died in 753 B.C., he was succeeded by his son, Zechariah, whose reign lasted only six months. Zechariah was murdered by Shallum.

THE LAST KINGS These three decades mark the decline and fall of the
753-723 B.C. Northern Kingdom as the Assyrian Kingdom extended its control into the land of Palestine. From its highest peak of commercial and political prosperity, Israel fell in this short period to a state of Assyrian vassalage.

A. Menahem and Pekahiah

Menahem ruled Israel for approximately ten years after Shallum's one-month rule ended in his assassination. Facing aggression by Tiglath-pileser III or Pul who ascended the Assyrian throne in 745 B.C., Menahem paid tribute in order to avoid invasion. Pekahiah, his son, maintained the same policy of subservience during his two-year rule.

B. Pekah, 739-731 B.C.

Pekah very likely led a movement of revolt against Assyria and was responsible for the assassination of Pekahiah. In Syria a new king, Rezin, provided aggressive leadership. Facing a common foe, these two kings formed an alliance to resist Assyria. Judah up to this time had provided aggressive leadership in resisting Assyria but in 735 Ahaz was enthroned in Jerusalem by a pro-Assyrian party. Although the Syro-- Israelite alliance tried to coerce Judah to support them by invading Judah (II Kings 16:5-9; II Chron. 28:5-15; Isa. 7:1—8:8), the attempt ended in failure. In 732 B.C., Tiglath-pileser conquered Syria by occupying Damascus. Rezin was killed. In Samaria, the Israelites killed Pekah and enthroned Hoshea as a vassal of the king of Assyria.

C. Hoshea the last king

When Shalmaneser V succeeded Tiglath-pileser III on the Assyrian throne, 727 B.C., Hoshea discontinued his tributary payments to Assyria depending on Egypt for help. By 726 the Assyrian king besieged Samaria. After a three-year siege Hoshea was forced to surrender. This ended the Northern Kingdom.

Under the Assyrian policy of scattering conquered people, 28,000 Israelites were taken captive and dispersed into the regions of Persia. In return, colonists from Babylonia were settled in Samaria and Israel was reduced to the status of an Assyrian province.

For over two centuries the Israelites had followed the pattern set by Jeroboam I who led his people into idolatry, breaking the first commandment in the Decalogue. Prophet after prophet warned the kings as well as the people of impending judgment. For their gross idolatry and their failure to heed the admonition to serve God, the Israelites were subjected to captivity (II Kings 17:1-23).

Guide Questions for Study and Discussion

1. By what other names was the Northern Kingdom known?
2. How did Ahijah inform Jeroboam that he would be a king?
3. Why was the prophet from Judah killed on his return trip?
4. Why did Baasha abandon his fortification of Ramah?
5. What did Omri do to establish Israel as a strong nation?
6. How did Ahab promote the religion of Baal?
7. How did Elijah oppose Ahab?
8. Why was the Northern Kingdom so weak under Jehu?
9. Who predicted the expansion of Israel under Jeroboam II?
10. What finally caused the fall of the Northern Kingdom?

Activities for Enrichment and Application

1. What leadership qualifications which Elijah and Elisha possessed led to spiritual interest on the part of the people?
2. Give evidences of the grace of God manifested toward the Northern Kingdom.
3. Trace the religious conditions throughout the period of the Northern Kingdom. Compare to those in the Southern Kingdom.
4. Show how God's power was manifested through the miracles performed by His prophets Elijah and Elisha during this period. What was the evident response to these? To what degree are miracles necessary if people are to follow God?

Significant Resources

FREE, JOSEPH P. *Archaeology and Bible History.* Wheaton, IL: Scripture Press, 1976.
SCHULTZ, SAMUEL J. *The Old Testament Speaks.* New York: Harper & Row, 1970.
THIELE, EDWIN R. *A Chronology of the Hebrew Kings.* Grand Rapids: Zondervan Pub. House, 1977.
WRIGHT, GEORGE E. *Biblical Archaeology.* Philadelphia: Westminster Press, 1963.

The Divided Kingdom Era, 931–586 B.C.

Date	NORTHERN KINGDOM Kings	Prophets	SOUTHERN KINGDOM Kings	FOREIGN KINGS
931	Jeroboam Dynasty		Rehoboam	Rezon[1]
	Jeroboam	Ahijah	Abijam	
		Shemaiah		
		Iddo		
	Nadab		Asa	
909	Baasha Dynasty		Azariah	
	Baasha		Hanani	
		Jehu		
	Elah			
	(Zimri)			
885	Omri Dynasty			
	Omri (Tibni)	Elijah	Jehoshaphat	Benhadad[1]
	Ahab	Micaiah	Eliezer	
	Ahaziah	Elisha	Jehoram	Shalmaneser III[2]
	Joram		Jehoiada	Ahaziah
841	Jehu Dynasty			
	Jehu		Athaliah	Hazael[1]
	Jehoahaz		Zechariah	Joash
	Jehoash	*Jonah*	*Joel**	Amaziah	Benhadad II [1]
	Jeroboam II	*Amos*	Azariah	
		Hosea		
	Zechariah			
752	Last Kings		Jotham	
	Shallum			
	Menahem		*Isaiah*	Tiglath-pileser III[2]
	Pekahiah		Ahaz	Rezin[1]
	Pekah	Oded		Shalmaneser V[2]
	Hoshea			
722	Fall of Samaria			Sargon II[2]
		Micah	Hezekiah	Sennacherib[2]
			Manasseh	Esarhaddon[2]
				Ashurbanipal[2]
		*Nahum**	Amon	
640		*Zephaniah**	Josiah	
		Jeremiah,		
		Huldah		
		*Habakkuk**		
			Jehoahaz	Nabopolassar[3]
				Nebuchad- nezzar[3]
			Jehoiakim	
			Jehoiachin	
		Daniel	Zedekiah	
		Ezekiel		
586			Fall of Jerusalem	

Note: Writing prophets are indicated by *italics*.
Obadiah,* Haggai, Zechariah, and Malachi
ministered after the Fall of Jerusalem.

* Approximate time.

[1]Syria
[2]Assyria
[3]Babylonia

CHAPTER TEN

The Kingdom of Judah

Rehoboam-Jotham

SCRIPTURE SURVEY: I Kings 12—22; II Kings 1—15; II Chronicles
10—27

EXTENT OF TIME: ca. 931-735 B.C.

Only two tribes remained loyal to the Davidic dynasty ruling in Jerusalem after the death of Solomon. Whereas ruling families and capitals changed frequently in the Northern Kingdom, the descendants of David with one exception retained continuous royal leadership in the capital city established by David.

Judah, also known as the Southern Kingdom, continued its established rule for nearly three and a half centuries beginning with Rehoboam the son of Solomon (931-586 B.C.). A total of twenty kings ruled in Judah during this period. Twelve of these were contemporary with the rulers in the Northern Kingdom.

This long period of Judah's history can conveniently be considered by focusing attention upon four kings who exerted outstanding leadership. For each of these kings we suggest an approximate date that highlights this period chronologically: [1]

Jehoshaphat	850 B.C.
Uzziah	750 B.C.
Hezekiah	700 B.C.
Josiah	630 B.C.

The biblical account of the Southern Kingdom is given in the books of I and II Kings in its relationship to the developments in the Northern Kingdom. Supplementary information is provided in II Chronicles which is primarily devoted to the history of the Davidic dynasty.

THE ERA OF JEHOSHAPHAT An abrupt change took place in Jerusalem after Solomon died in 931 B.C. Rehoboam faced rebellion and a disruption of the great empire that he inherited. Numerous leaders—Jeroboam in the northern tribes, Rezon in Damascus, and Hadad in Edom—championed the cause of their own people and chal-

---

[1] For chronological description of the kings of Israel and Judah, see chart, "Old Testament Kings and Prophets" by John Whitcomb (Winona Lake, Ind.: Grace Theological Seminary), rev. 1962.

lenged the rule of the Solomonic successor.

A. Cause of disruption

Two reasons are given in Scripture for the termination of the union of Israel that had been established by David. The northern tribes rebelled against the excessive taxation and the threat of heavier levies by Rehoboam. Explicitly, the biblical narrative also points to Solomon's apostasy and idolatry as a cause for divine judgment (I Kings 11:9-13). For David's sake this division did not occur until after the death of Solomon (II Sam. 7:12-16).

Rehoboam made plans to suppress the Israelite rebellion. When he called for troops, only the tribes of Judah and Benjamin responded to support him. A prophet Shemaiah advised Rehoboam not to fight against the seceding tribes. In the early years of his reign, Rehoboam was further humbled by an invasion by Shishak the ruler of Egypt. Shemaiah assured the leaders of Judah that they would not be destroyed, even though the Egyptians raided Jerusalem and appropriated some of the temple treasures.

Although Rehoboam apparently began his reign with sincere religious devotion, he soon succumbed to prevailing idolatrous influences. His seventeen-year reign and the short three-year rule of his son Abijam were characterized by apostasy and idolatry, even though the service of God in the temple was·maintained. The prophet Iddo may have warned these kings of their sinful ways.

B. Asa's reforms

Asa's forty-one-year reign (910-869 B.C.) prepared the way for the religious revival that prevailed under Jehoshaphat. Asa began a program of reform, admonishing the people to keep the Mosaic Law. When attacked by the Ethiopians from the south, Asa repulsed them with divine aid. Admonished by the prophet Azariah, King Asa removed idols throughout the land, crushed and burned the image of Asherah the Canaanite goddess of fertility in the valley of Kidron, and removed Maacah as queen mother.

When the religious celebrations in Jerusalem attracted the people from the Northern Kingdom, Baasha began to fortify Ramah, five miles north of Jerusalem. Fearing this as a military threat, Asa sent a bribe to Benhadad, king of Syria. When Syria seized Israelite territory in the north, Baasha withdrew his forces from Ramah.

For this alliance with Syria, the king of Judah was severely rebuked by a prophet named Hanani. Asa should have trusted God instead of depending upon the help of a heathen king. Unfortunately Asa did not respond favorably to God's warning, for he imprisoned the prophet. Two years before his death, Asa was stricken by a fatal disease.

THE REIGN OF The twenty-five-year reign of Jehoshaphat (872-848
JEHOSHAPHAT B.C.) was one of the most encouraging and helpful eras
in the religious history of Judah. Since Jehoshaphat was
thirty-five years old when he began to reign, he very likely had, during the
early years of his life, come under the influence of Judah's great religious leaders. Under a well-organized program he sent princes, priests,
and Levites throughout the land to teach the people the Law.

Internationally this was a period of peace. The Philistines and Arabs
acknowledged the superiority of Judah by bringing presents and tribute
to Jehoshaphat. This enabled the king of Judah to build fortresses and
store cities throughout the land where he stationed military units. In addition, he had five army commanders in Jerusalem who were directly
responsible to him.

When Jehoshaphat was threatened by a terrifying invasion of Moabites
and Edomites from the southeast, he proclaimed a fast in all the cities
of Judah. In the court of the temple the king himself led a prayer ex-
pressing his faith in God in the simple words "neither know we what to
do; but our eyes are upon thee." Through Jahaziel, a Levite of the sons
of Asaph, the assembly received the divine assurance that even without
fighting they should see a great victory. When Judah marched toward the
enemy, they were thrown into confusion and massacred each other. After
collecting spoils for three days, Jehoshaphat led his people triumphantly
back to Jerusalem and the fear of God fell on the nations round about.

A. Alliance with the Omride dynasty

Friendly relations prevailed between Judah and Israel during the days
of Jehoshaphat. For his alliance with the godless ruling family in the
Northern Kingdom, Jehoshaphat was severely rebuked on numerous occasions. Very likely this affinity between these two royal families began
early in Jehoshaphat's reign, sealing the alliance in the marriage of his
son Jehoram [2] with Athaliah, the daughter of Ahab and Jezebel. Even
though this relationship with the Omride dynasty provided Judah with
a friendly nation to the north as a protection from other nations, Jehoshaphat was rebuked by at least four prophets.

B. Micaiah

Before Israel and Judah joined in the battle against Syria in which Ahab
was killed, Jehoshaphat had an uneasy conscience when the 400 Israelite

---

[2] In this study, the son of Jehoshaphat is designated by the name Jehoram and the
son of Ahab is designated as Joram, even though the two are used interchangeably
in Scripture.

prophets predicted success in this venture. To pacify Jehoshaphat, the prophet Micaiah was called before the kings, solemnly warning that the king of Israel would be killed (I Kings 22). Jehoshaphat narrowly escaped death.

C. Jehu the prophet

When Jehoshaphat returned to Jerusalem from this battle, he was confronted by Jehu with the words: "Shouldest thou help the ungodly, and love them that hate the Lord?" (II Chron. 19:2).

D. Eliezer

After Ahab's death, Jehoshaphat continued his affinity with Israel in an alliance with Ahaziah the son of Ahab. Together these kings launched ships at Ezion-geber for commercial purposes. In accordance with the prediction of the prophet Eliezer these ships were wrecked (II Chron. 20:35-37).

E. Elisha

When Joram, the son of Ahab who succeeded Ahaziah on the throne of Israel, attempted to suppress Moab, Jehoshaphat joined in this military venture. When the armies of Judah, Israel, and Edom were in a desperate condition for lack of water, the prophet Elisha appeared before the three kings in charge. In the presence of this prophet, Jehoshaphat was once more made conscious of the fact that he was in an alliance with ungodly kings (II Kings 3:1-27).

Within a decade the results of Jehoshaphat's policy of ungodly alliances unfolded in Judah. When Jehoshaphat died in 848 B.C., Jehoram as king not only executed six of his brothers but also espoused the sinful ways of Ahab and Jezebel. This change in religion may reasonably be attributed to Athaliah. According to II Chronicles 21:11-15, Elijah the prophet severely reproached Jehoram, who died in 841 B.C. of an incurable disease.

Ahaziah the son of Jehoram ruled less than a year. Visiting his uncle Joram the son of Ahab, Ahaziah was killed by Jehu who exterminated the Omride dynasty and began to reign in Samaria. In Jerusalem, Athaliah the mother of Ahaziah seized the Davidic throne and began a six-year reign of terror. To secure her position, she began the execution of the royal family. What Jezebel had done to the prophets in Israel, Athaliah did to the royal family to whom the Davidic promise had been made of an eternal throne (II Sam. 7:12-16). Providentially, a son Joash was saved and the Davidic dynasty was restored after the execution of Athaliah.

THE ERA OF Joash was enthroned at the age of seven in 835 B.C. and
UZZIAH reigned until 796 B.C. During the early decades of his
(AZARIAH) reign, Joash was guided and influenced by Jehoiada, a
priest who was responsible for his enthronement. The
temple with its services had suffered under the three preceding rulers
but was now restored. However, when Jehoiada died, apostasy swept the
kingdom of Judah so extensively that when Zechariah, the son of Jehoiada,
warned the people that they would not prosper if they continued to dis-
obey the commandments of the Lord, he was stoned in the court of the
temple.

Joash was threatened by Syrian aggression. When the Syrians conquered Gath, Joash stripped the temple of its dedicated treasures and sent
them to Hazael to avoid invasion. Presumably, failure to pay tribute
brought the Syrian armies to Jerusalem after the turn of the century.
Judah's capital was invaded and before the Syrians left with the spoils,
they killed some of the princes and wounded Joash, who was subsequently
slain by his palace servants. This judgment came upon the king who permitted apostasy to permeate Judah and even tolerated the shedding of
innocent blood.

A. Amaziah

Amaziah, who is credited with a total of twenty-nine-years' rule
(796-767 B.C.), actually ruled only a short period. Uzziah apparently
was made coregent with his father in 791.

The death of Hazael in Damascus at the turn of the century provided
relief from Syrian aggression for the kingdom of Judah as well as Israel.
Amaziah developed his military strength sufficiently to recover control
over Edom. Proud of his military victory, he challenged Jehoash of Israel
to a battle. As a result Judah was invaded by the Israelites who not only
plundered Jerusalem but also broke down part of the wall and took
royal hostages. King Amaziah was also captured and probably held captive in Israel until 782 when Jehoash died.[3]

B. The reign of Uzziah or Azariah

When Amaziah broke the peace that had existed between Judah and
Israel for almost a hundred years, the national hopes of the Southern
Kingdom sank to the lowest point since the division of Solomon's Kingdom. Apparently Uzziah was made coregent in 791 and guided the affairs
of state during the remainder of Amaziah's reign, assuming full control
in 767 when his father was assassinated.

Gradually but constructively Uzziah initiated policies that brought

---

[3] For a more extensive treatment of these developments, see Schultz, *The Old
Testament Speaks*, pp. 203-205.

about the restoration of Judah. Very likely he rebuilt the walls of Jerusalem. Judah's vassalage to Israel must have terminated, at the latest, with Amaziah's death or perhaps with his release fifteen years earlier. Apparently a policy of friendliness and cooperation prevailed between Jeroboam II and Uzziah.

With a program of military preparedness and economic expansion, Uzziah brought the Philistines, the Edomites, and Ammonites under his control, extending Judah's borders to the Gulf of Aqaba. Throughout the kingdom, he provided wells needed for large herds in desert areas and erected towers for the protection of vinedressers as they expanded their production. Copper and iron mining industries, which had flourished under Solomon, were revived in the Sinai Peninsula. Judah's growth and influence during this period were second only to those experienced in Davidic and Solomonic times.

Uzziah's prosperity was directly related to his dependence upon God (II Chron. 26:5, 7). Zechariah, a prophet otherwise unknown, effectively instructed the king who until about 750 B.C. had a wholesome and humble attitude toward God. At the height of his success, however, Uzziah assumed that he could enter the temple and burn incense. With the support of eighty priests, the high priest whose name was Azariah confronted Uzziah with the fact that this was the prerogative of those consecrated for this purpose (cf. Ex. 30:7; Num. 18:1-7). In anger the king defied the priests. As a result of divine judgment, Uzziah became leprous. For the rest of his reign he was ostracized from the palace and denied ordinary social privileges. He could not even enter the temple. Jotham was made coruler in 750 B.C. and assumed the royal responsibilities for the remainder of his father's life.

With the death of Jeroboam in 753, the Southern Kingdom that had been so solidly built under Uzziah emerged as the strongest power in Canaan. Very likely Uzziah cherished hopes of restoring the whole Solomonic empire to Judah, but these were soon shattered by the rising power of Assyria. When Tiglath-pileser III of Assyria began in 745 B.C. to move his armies westward, Azariah the king of Judah is mentioned as leading the opposition. In the meantime, Menahem in behalf of Israel paid tribute to the Assyrian king.

Jotham assumed sole control of Judah when Uzziah died in 740 B.C. This marked a crucial year in the history of Judah when the king died who restored Judah from its vassalage to Israel and made it the most powerful nation in Palestine. The impending threat of Assyrian invasion clouded the future national hopes. This was also the year in which Isaiah was called to be the prophet of God in Jerusalem. Jotham continued an anti-Assyrian policy as he assumed the leadership of Judah, but in 735 B.C. a pro-Assyrian party elevated Jotham's son Ahaz to the throne.

Guide Questions for Study and Discussion

1. How does the account in Kings differ from the account in Chronicles?
2. What were the causes of the disruption of the Solomonic kingdom when Rehoboam became king?
3. What did Asa do to promote a religious revival?
4. Why was Jehoshaphat concerned about joining Ahab in battle?
5. Whose influence did Athaliah reflect when she reigned in Judah?
6. How did the influence of Jehoiada affect the Kingdom of Judah?
7. How did the aggressive policies of Hazael in Syria affect Judah?
8. How did Uzziah establish Judah economically?
9. Why was Uzziah smitten with leprosy?
10. What was Uzziah's policy toward Assyria?

Activities for Enrichment and Application

1. Compare the religious influence of Jehoshaphat in Judah and in Israel. What dangers of association or friendship with the ungodly are seen in Jehoshaphat's experience?
2. How were the central movements in this study directly resultant from failure to keep the commands of God? What one commandment was consistently broken? Do world kings and leaders face similar situations today? What words of warning do they need from God's messengers?
3. Trace the evidences of the grace of God manifested toward the Southern Kingdom.
4. What was the extent of influence the prophets exercised over the kings studied in this chapter? To what degree should the clergy influence politicians?
5. List the Messianic line of kings in the Southern Kingdom.

Significant Resources

BEECHER, WILLIS J. "Chronicles" in *The International Standard Bible Encyclopedia.* Vol. I. Ed. by James Orr. Grand Rapids: Wm. B. Eerdmans Pub. Co., 1955.

EDERSHEIM, ALFRED. *Old Testament Bible History.* Grand Rapids: Wm. B. Eerdmans Pub. Co., 1972.

FREEMAN, HOBART E. *An Introduction to the Old Testament Prophets.* Chicago: Moody Press, 1968.

PAYNE, J. BARTON. *Encyclopedia of Biblical Prophecy.* New York: Harper & Row, 1973.

CHAPTER ELEVEN

The Kingdom of Judah

Ahaz-Zedekiah

SCRIPTURE SURVEY: II Kings 16:1—25:7; II Chronicles 28:1—36:21
EXTENT OF TIME: ca. 735-586 B.C.
Hezekiah and Josiah are the best-known kings during the last century and
a half (735-586 B.C.) of Judah's existence as a kingdom. Both kings were
reformers who took the initiative in leading their people back to God
and postponing the judgment announced by the prophets upon Jerusalem.

AHAZ—FATHER   The nations in Palestine were on the verge of being
OF HEZEKIAH   overrun by the Assyrian armies when Ahaz was enthroned (735 B.C.) in Jerusalem by a pro-Assyrian
party in the kingdom of Judah. Simultaneously, Pekah in Israel and
Rezin in Syria formed an anti-Assyrian alliance. To secure themselves
against attack from the south, these two kings waged the Syro-Ephraimite
war against Judah, taking thousands of Judeans captive. Warned by a
prophet named Oded, the king of Israel released the prisoners of war.

A. Isaiah's warning

When Ahaz was faced with the threat of invasion, Isaiah was sent to
meet him with the admonition to place his trust in God with the assurance
that the two kings from the north would be dethroned (Isa. 7—9). Ignoring and defying Isaiah, the king of Judah appealed to Tiglath-pileser,
the king of Assyria, for aid. This brought immediate results. As a result
of Assyrian aggression, the kingdom of Syria was terminated with the
death of Rezin, and Israel was made tributary with Hoshea, replacing
Pekah in 732 B.C. Ahaz himself met the Assyrian king in Damascus,
participating with him in pagan religious rites and pledging his loyalty.

B. Ahaz' continued idolatry and eventual death

Ahaz promoted the most obnoxious idolatrous practices. Taking the
measurements of the altar in Damascus, Ahaz ordered Urijah the priest
to duplicate this altar in the temple in Jerusalem. Ahaz took the lead in
pagan worship, had his son walk through the fire according to heathen
customs, and took treasures from the temple to meet the demands of the
Assyrian king. Even though he guided his nation successfully through

this period of international crises, he incurred God's wrath. In subsequent periods, the Assyrian power extended into Judah like a razor in God's hand (Isa. 7:20), and like a river (Isa. 8:7), according to the prediction of Isaiah.

HEZEKIAH—   When Hezekiah began his reign in 716 B.C. in
A RIGHTEOUS KING Jerusalem, the Northern Kingdom had already
                   capitulated to the Assyrian advance with the fall
of Samaria in 722. Throughout his twenty-nine-year reign, Hezekiah projected a reversal of the political and religious policies his wicked father had initiated.

With a keen realization that Israel's captivity was the consequence of a broken covenant and disobedience to God (II Kings 18:9-12), Hezekiah placed his confidence in God as he began an effective reform. Levites were called in to repair and cleanse the temple for worship, idols were removed, vessels were sanctified, and sacrifices were initiated accompanied by liturgical singing. In an attempt to heal the religious breach that had prevailed between the two kingdoms since Solomon's death, Hezekiah sent invitations to the people of the northern tribes to participate in the observance of the Passover in Jerusalem. At no time since the dedication of the temple had Jerusalem experienced such a joyful celebration. Even the bronze serpent erected by Moses (Num. 21:4-9), used by the people as an object of worship, was destroyed.

Politically, Hezekiah acknowledged the overlordship of Sargon II (721-705 B.C.), since Judah had already been committed to Assyrian vassalage under Ahaz. This policy averted interference in Judah when Sargon dispatched his troops to Ashdod, west of Jerusalem in 711 B.C. (Isa. 20:1). In the meantime, Hezekiah concentrated on a construction defense program, organizing and equipping his army. To assure Jerusalem of an adequate water supply in case of a prolonged siege, Hezekiah constructed a tunnel connecting the Siloam pool with the spring of Gihon. Through 1,777 feet of solid rock, the Judean engineers channeled fresh water into the pool of Siloam which was also constructed at this time. Ever since its discovery in 1880, when the inscription on it was deciphered, the Siloam tunnel has been an attraction for tourists. The wall of Jerusalem was also extended to enclose the Siloam pool. Although Hezekiah did all in his power to prepare for an Assyrian invasion, he did not depend only upon human resources but publicly expressed his dependence upon God before his people assembled in the city square in these words: "With him is an arm of flesh; but with us is the Lord our God to help us and to fight our battles" (II Chron. 32:8).

With the accession of Sennacherib to the Assyrian throne in 705, rebellions broke out in many parts of the Assyrian empire. In 701 Sennacherib marched his armies into Palestine, boasting in his own records that he conquered 46 walled cities in the maritime plain. After exacting a large tribute from Hezekiah, the king of Assyria demanded the surrender of Jerusalem. Encouraged by Isaiah, Hezekiah placed his trust in God for deliverance. Before Sennacherib could fulfill his threat, he received word of a revolt in Babylon. Immediately he rushed back east, boasting that he had taken 200,000 prisoners but simply noting that Hezekiah had been shut up like a bird in a cage.

This successful resistance in 701 brought to Hezekiah the acclaim and recognition of the surrounding nations expressed in abundant gifts (II Chron. 32:23). Not least among those sending congratulations was Merodach-baladan of Babylon who also had heard of Hezekiah's recovery from a severe illness. After Hezekiah displayed his wealth to the Babylonian embassy, the prophet Isaiah warned the king of Judah of impending judgment on Jerusalem, but tempered his warning by the assurance that he would have a period of peace during his reign.

Sennacherib did not conclude his efforts to suppress rebellions in the Tigris-Euphrates area until he destroyed Babylon in 689 B.C. Hearing about Tirhakah (II Kings 19:9ff.), he directed his interests westward once more. This time he sent letters to Hezekiah with an ultimatum to surrender. Hezekiah, who had experienced a previous deliverance and since then had enjoyed over a decade of peace and prosperity, calmly but confidently spread these letters before the Lord as he prayed in the temple. Isaiah sent words of assurance. The Assyrian armies never reached Jerusalem, but were destroyed somewhere en route—possibly in the Arabian Desert. Sennacherib returned to Nineveh, where he was killed by two of his sons in 681 B.C.

Hezekiah, unlike a number of his predecessors, was buried in honor when he died in 686 B.C. Not only had he led his people in the greatest reformation in Judah's history, but he had also given religious leadership to many people from the northern tribes.

JOSIAH'S PREDECESSORS Nearly one-half a century passed between the end of Hezekiah's reign and the enthronement of Josiah (686-640 B.C.). Manasseh, who had been made coregent with his father in 696, reigned until 642 when he was succeeded by his son Amon.

A. Manasseh

Manasseh plunged Judah into its darkest era of idolatry by erecting altars to Baal and constructing idols comparable only to Ahab and Jezebel in the Northern Kingdom. Star and planetary worship was instituted, the Ammonite deity Moloch was acknowledged by the Hebrew king in the sacrifice of children in the Hinnom Valley, and astrology, divination, and occultism were officially sanctioned. In open defiance of God, altars for worshiping the host of heaven were placed in the courts of the temple, while graven images of Asherah, the wife of Baal, were placed in the temple itself. It is quite likely that tradition is correct in attributing the martyrdom of Isaiah to Manasseh, since he shed much innocent blood (II Kings 21:16). Morally and religiously, Judah reached a very low point under this wicked king.

During Manasseh's reign, Esarhaddon and Ashurbanipal extended Assyrian control down to Thebes in Egypt by 663 B.C. Although the date for Manasseh's captivity (II Chron. 33:10-13) is not given, it is likely that he was taken to Babylon during the last decade of his reign. Being returned after his repentance, Manasseh probably had little time to reverse the idolatrous influence he had promoted throughout the kingdom during his earlier years.

B. Amon

Idolatry prevailed under Manasseh's son Amon. The early training of Amon had made a decidedly greater impact upon him than the belated period of reformation. Before two years of his reign had passed, Amon was slain by slaves in the palace. Although his reign was brief, his godless leadership provided opportunity for Judah to revert to terrible apostasy.

JOSIAH National and international changes of great significance occurred during the thirty-one-year reign of Josiah. Politically, the Assyrian empire gave way with the death of Ashurbanipal in 633 and the destruction of Nineveh in 612 B.C. to the rising kingdoms of Media and Babylon. Religiously Josiah brought about the last great reformation before the destruction of Judah.

A. Religious reformation

As an eight-year-old boy Josiah was suddenly elevated to the Davidic throne in Jerusalem after the death of his father. In all likelihood Josiah had been instructed by godly teachers and priests. When he was sixteen, he began to seek God earnestly and in four more years (628 B.C.), his devotion to God had crystallized to the point that he began a religious reformation. In 621 B.C. while the temple was being repaired, the book of the Law was recovered and the Passover was observed in a manner unprecedented in the history of Judah. Politically it was also safe to remove any religious practices associated with Assyria at this time since Assyrian influence was waning. Very likely Josiah continued to give religious leadership in leading his people back to God until the end of his reign.

B. Huldah

When the Law was discovered in the temple, Huldah the prophetess was called in by the king. She warned the king of impending judgment and instructed him in his responsibilities to obey the Law. Since Manasseh had shed so much innocent blood, it is probable that he destroyed as many of the existing copies of the Law of Moses as he could find so that the contents of the Law were relatively unknown until this copy was made available to the king of Judah.

C. Jeremiah

Jeremiah was called to the prophetic ministry in 627 B.C. Since Josiah had already begun his reform, it is reasonable to conclude that Jeremiah and Josiah worked hand in hand. Living in Anathoth, Jeremiah may not have been available or even acquainted with Josiah when the book of the Law was found in 621. However, the first twenty chapters of Jeremiah may largely be related to the Josian era.

D. Sudden death

The destruction of the Assyrian capital Nineveh in 612 B.C. by the Medo-Babylonian coalition affected the entire Fertile Crescent. In a state of military preparedness, Josiah made his fatal mistake by rushing his armies up to Megiddo attempting to stop Necho, king of Egypt, from aiding the remnant of the Assyrian army at Haran. Josiah was fatally wounded and the Judean army was routed. Suddenly the national and international hopes of Judah vanished as the thirty-nine-year-old king was entombed in the city of David. After eighteen years of intimate association with Josiah, the great prophet is singled out by name in II Chronicles 35:25—"and Jeremiah lamented for Josiah."

THE LAST KINGS   Rapid changes took place during the next quarter of
OF JUDAH   a century, resulting in the destruction of Jerusalem.
Although Assyria which had dominated Palestine for more than a century had fallen, the Babylonian kingdom emerged as the controlling power under which the Kingdom of Judah was absorbed.

A. Jehoiakim, 609-598 B.C.

Before Jehoahaz had ruled three months in Jerusalem, the king of Egypt returned from Carchemish, where he had halted the Babylonian advance, and placed Jehoiakim, another son of Josiah, on the Davidic throne. Jehoahaz was taken prisoner to Egypt and died there as predicted by Jeremiah (22:11, 12).

Jehoiakim was subject to Egypt until 605 B.C. when the Necho was defeated by the Babylonians in the battle of Carchemish. That summer the Babylonian armies advanced south and claimed treasures and hostages in Jerusalem, among whom were Daniel and his friends. By 598 B.C. Jehoiakim apparently maintained an anti-Babylonian policy so that Nebuchadnezzar marched his armies to Jerusalem. Jehoiakim seems to have been killed by marauding Chaldean bands supported by Moabites, Ammonites, and Syrians before the Babylonian forces reached Palestine. Young Jehoiachin, son of Jehoiakim, ruled only three months. Realizing that it was futile to resist the Babylonian forces besieging Jerusalem, Jehoiachin surrendered to Nebuchadnezzar. This time the invaders stripped the temple and the royal treasuries and took the king, the queen mother, palace officials, executives, artisans, and community leaders captive. Not least among the thousands was Ezekiel. Zedekiah, the youngest son of Josiah, was made puppet king and left in charge of Judah.[1]

B. Zedekiah, 597-586 B.C.

Subject to the Babylonians, Zedekiah was able to maintain the kingdom of Judah for only eleven years. He was under constant pressure to join the Egyptians in a rebellion against the Babylonians. When Zedekiah yielded to the pro-Egyptian party, the Babylonian armies advanced to Jerusalem besieging it in 588. After several years Jerusalem was conquered, the temple was reduced to ashes, and the capital of Judah was abandoned as its citizens were taken captive or dispersed. Zedekiah escaped but was captured at Jericho and taken to Riblah. After the execution of his sons, Zedekiah was blinded and taken in chains to Babylon.

C. Jeremiah's ministry

Jeremiah served as a faithful messenger of God through the hectic decades that brought the Kingdom of Judah to its doom. During Jehoiakim's reign, Jeremiah's scroll was burned by the king. When Jeremiah announced the destruction of the temple (Jer. 7, 26), the people would have executed him had it not been for Ahikam, a prominent political figure who came to defend him.

Throughout the last decade, Jeremiah constantly advised the vascillating king to be subservient to the Babylonian king. Being left with the lower classes of people, Jeremiah was subjected to persecution and frequent suffering as he warned the people of judgment to come, withstood the false prophets in Jerusalem, and advised the exiles by correspondence

---

[1] Note the alternate names for these last kings:
Jehoahaz—Shallum
Jehoiakim — Eliakim
Jehoiachin — Coniah or Jeconiah
Zedekiah—Mattaniah

that they should not believe the false prophets who were active there, encouraging them in the hope of an immediate return to Jerusalem. Even though Jeremiah was imprisoned, thrown in a dungeon, and abandoned by his people, he was sustained by God to live with his people through the destruction of Jerusalem. At the end of a forty-year ministry, he witnessed the disintegration of the Davidic kingdom and the destruction of the Solomonic temple which had been the pride and glory of Israel for almost four centuries. The book of Lamentations may well express the reflections of Jeremiah as he saw the ruins of his beloved city of Jerusalem.

Guide Questions for Study and Discussion

1. Who were the participants in the Syro-Ephraimitic war?
2. How did Ahaz avoid an invasion by Assyria?
3. What was Ahaz' attitude toward Isaiah?
4. What preparation did Hezekiah make for defending his nation?
5. How did Isaiah help Hezekiah in 701 when Sennacherib demanded the surrender of Jerusalem?
6. Why did Sennacherib return so suddenly to Babylon in 701 B.C.?
7. How was Sennacherib defeated in his second attempt to subject Hezekiah?
8. What were the religious policies of Manasseh?
9. How did international developments aid Josiah in his religious reformation?
10. Why did Nebuchadnezzar destroy Jerusalem?

Activities for Enrichment and Application

1. Trace the Assyro-Judah relationship during the reign of Hezekiah. Point out the evidence of divine intervention and direction in this relationship. Evaluate the influence of the prophet Isaiah in the central events. Illustrate the degree to which Christian statesmen are influencing world events today.
2. Outline the progress in Josiah's religious reformation. Point out the relationship between Josiah's reforms and his understanding of and attitude toward God and the Law of God. What present-day reforms might result from the reading and applying of God's Word by the people of your commuity?
3. Summarize the ministry of Jeremiah during the last forty years of Judah's history. Discuss the Christian's responsibility in governmental affairs.
4. List the most significant international events between 650-586 B.C. Discuss the relationship of these events to prophecy and to the violation of God's covenant with His chosen people (cf. Deut. 29, 30).

Significant Resources

HARRISON, ROLAND K. *Jeremiah and Lamentations*. Downers Grove, IL: InterVarsity Press, 1973.
SCHULTZ, SAMUEL J. *The Old Testament Speaks*. New York: Harper & Row, 1970.

CHAPTER TWELVE

Beyond the Exile

SCRIPTURE SURVEY: Ezra, Esther, Nehemiah
EXTENT OF TIME: ca. 539-425 B.C.
Little is known about the conditions of the Jewish people who were taken into Babylonian exile. In the Biblical narrative, the period from the destruction of Jerusalem in 586 B.C. to the return of the exiles beginning in 538 B.C. is passed in silence. The books of Ezra, Esther, and Nehemiah provide some insight into the activities of God's chosen people from the time of their return to the end of the Old Testament era, the days of Nehemiah and Malachi (ca. 450-400 B.C.).

Chronologically this material may be conveniently divided into four periods:

I. Jerusalem Reestablished, ca. 539-515 B.C.	Ezra 1—6
II. Esther the Queen, ca. 483 B.C.	Esther 1—10
III. Ezra the Reformer, ca. 457 B.C.	Ezra 7—10
IV. Nehemiah the Governor, ca. 444 B.C.	Nehemiah 1—13

Jewish captivity had been foretold by Isaiah, Micah, Jeremiah, and other prophets for many generations. The exiles, who were conscious of the fact that their captivity came as God's judgment upon a sinful nation, expeiienced a deep sense of humiliation and anguish of soul[1] The prophets likewise held out the promise of restoration. Noteworthy among the predictions were the messages by Jeremiah (25:11, 12; 29:10) that the captivity would be terminated in seventy years and the designation by Isaiah that Cyrus would be the shepherd used by God to allow the Jews to return (Isa. 44:28).

JERUSALEM The first six chapters of Ezra provide a brief account **REESTABLISHED** of the developments associated with the experiences of the exiles who return to rebuild the temple. Almost twenty-five years passed before they realized their hopes.

---

[1] Historical evidence seems to be lacking to support the idea that the Jewish captives were mistreated physically or suppressed in their civic and religious activities during the days of Babylonian supremacy. Cf. C. F. Whitley, *The Exilic Age* (London: Westminster Press, 1957), p. 79.

A. The return, Ezra 1—2

When Cyrus as king of Persia conquered Babylon, he issued a decree which allowed the Jews to return. This was a reversal of the policy initiated by Tiglath-pileser of Assyria in 745 B.C. to deport conquered people. Cyrus permitted displaced persons to return to their homelands. Thousands of Jewish exiles prepared to leave Babylon. Loaded with vessels that Nebuchadnezzar had taken from the temple and with the approval and official support of King Cyrus, approximately 50,000 exiles successfully made the long trek to Jerusalem in 538 B.C. Outstanding among the eleven leaders mentioned were Zerubbabel, a grandson of Jehoiachin of the royal Davidic line, and Joshua (Jeshua) who served as the high priest officiating in religious matters.

B. Settlement at Jerusalem, 3—4

Upon arrival, the Jews immediately erected an altar and instituted worship, offering burnt offerings as prescribed by Moses (Ex. 29:38 ff.). On the fifteenth day of the seventh month they observed the Feast of Tabernacles (Lev. 23:34 ff.). In the atmosphere of these celebrations and festivities, plans were made for the people to provide money and produce for the masons and carpenters who negotiated with the Phoenicians for materials to build the temple.

Construction was begun in the second month of the next year. Antiphonal singing and triumphant praise by the new generation accompanied the ceremony of laying the foundation of the temple. The older people who remembered the glory and beauty of the Solomonic temple wept bitterly and unashamedly. Before long, the people from Samaria expressed their interest in this building program. Being denied participation, they responded with hostility and successfully hindered the work on the temple until 520 B.C.

C. The new temple, 5—6

In the second year of Darius, the new ruler in Persia, the Jews were able to resume their building project. The prophets Haggai and Zechariah were instrumental in stirring up the people to a renewed effort. This time Tattenai and his associates were not only forbidden to interfere, but were under orders of Darius to allot royal revenue from the province of Syria to the Jews for the temple.

The temple was completed in five years (520-515 B.C.).[2] After the impressive dedication ceremonies, the priests and Levites instituted their regular services in the sanctuary as prescribed for them in the Law of Moses. Thus the hopes of the returning exiles were realized.

---

[2]The events of the book of Haggai took place during this time.

THE STORY OF ESTHER   The book of Esther relates the experiences
of some of the Jews who remained in the land
of their exile instead of returning to Jerusalem. Historically, Esther is
identified with the reign of Xerxes or Ahasuerus, king of Persia (485-
465 B.C.). Although the name of God is not mentioned in this book,
divine providence and supernatural care are apparent throughout.

A. Jews at the Persian court, Esther 1—2

When Xerxes suddenly ostracized Queen Vashti by his royal decree, a
young Jewish orphan named Esther was crowned queen of Persia. Mordecai, a cousin who had formerly adopted Esther, was subsequently
instrumental in uncovering a plot in which two guards conspired to take
the king's life. Through Esther these plans were reported and the culprits
were hanged. In the official chronicle Mordecai was credited with saving
the Persian ruler's life.

B. Threat to the Jewish people, 3—5

When Haman, a Persian official, was advanced in rank by the king, he
was duly honored by everyone except Mordecai, who as a Jew refused to
do obeisance. In revenge Haman planned the execution of the Jews with
the endorsement of the king.

Mordecai in the meantime alerted his people who responded with fasting and mourning. Warning Esther that she possibly had come to the
kingdom for such a time as this (Esther 4:14), Mordecai prevailed upon
Esther to intercede before the king in behalf of the Jewish people. Consequently, she invited the king and Haman for dinner on two successive
days, making her request known on the second engagement.

C. Triumph of the Jews, 6—10

The night after the first dinner the king could not sleep. To pass the
time he requested to have the royal chronicles read to him through which
he learned that Mordecai had never been honored for saving the king's
life. Upon inquiry by the king, Haman outlined the procedure for honoring a man whom the king wanted to honor, anticipating that he would be
the recipient. Haman was shocked when he was ordered to honor
Mordecai for whom he had in the meantime erected gallows of execution
to be used on the day set for the fate of the Jews.

At the second banquet Esther forthrightly identified Haman as the
culprit. In consequence, Haman was hanged on the gallows he had prepared for Mordecai. The Jews were authorized to resist their enemies. In
the fighting that broke out, thousands of non-Jews were slain. Peace was
restored and the Jews celebrated their deliverance. In commemoration of
this deliverance, the Feast of Purim was observed annually.

EZRA THE REFORMER   The activities of Ezra himself are given in the last four chapters in the book bearing his name. He returned to Jerusalem in 457 B.C.

A. From Babylonia to Jerusalem, Ezra 7—8

Ezra was a ready scribe and student of the Law of Moses. In response to his appeal to Artaxerxes, Ezra was commissioned by this Persian king to lead a movement of Jews back to the province of Judah.

Elaborate preparation was made for this venture. Generous royal contributions, freewill offerings contributed by the exiles, and vessels for sacred use were given to Ezra for the Jerusalem temple. Provincial rulers beyond the Euphrates were ordered to supply Ezra with food and money lest the royal family incur the wrath of Israel's God. Ashamed to ask the king for police protection, Ezra assembled his people for prayer and fasting to appeal to God for divine aid as they embarked on the long and treacherous trek of nearly a thousand miles to Jerusalem. Three and a half months later they arrived in Jerusalem.

B. Reformation, 9—10

When Ezra learned that many of the Israelites were guilty of intermarriage with heathen inhabitants—even civil and religious leaders in Judah—he immediately took steps to correct these social evils. He called for a public assembly in the temple square and faced the congregation with the seriousness of their offense. After a three-month examination of the guilty parties, a sacrifice was made for a guilt offering with a solemn pledge by the offenders to annul their marriages.

NEHEMIAH THE GOVERNOR   Emerging as one of the most colorful figures in the postexilic era was Nehemiah who came to Jerusalem in 444 B.C. He forfeited his own position in the Persian court to serve his people in rebuilding Jerusalem. The book bearing his name may be conveniently considered under the headings given below.

A. Commissioned by Artaxerxes, Nehemiah 1:1—2:8

Serving as cupbearer to the Persian king, Nehemiah was greatly concerned about helping his people. After prayer and confession of the sins of his people, Nehemiah was able to make his request known when the king enquired about his personal welfare. In response, the king commissioned him to go to Jerusalem and serve as governor.

B. The Jerusalem mission, 2:9—6:19

Upon arrival, Nehemiah immediately made a tour of Jerusalem by night to inspect and appraise the conditions. Immediately he organized the people who responded enthusiastically in rebuilding the walls of the city. This sudden and intense activity aroused the opposition of the Arabs, the Ammonites, and the Ashdodites led by Geshem, Tobiah, and Sanballat. Nehemiah and his people not only prayed but by an intensive organized effort they guarded against attack and worked from dawn to dark to complete the walls.

Economically the people were hard pressed in paying their taxes, interest, and in support of their families. Calling a public assembly, Nehemiah announced an economic policy cancelling interest payments. Nehemiah himself set the example by not taking any governmental allowance in food and money during his twelve years of service.

Although the enemies of Nehemiah tried devious ways to ensnare Nehemiah, they failed repeatedly. Praying that God might strengthen him to withstand these efforts and keeping constant vigil, he was able to counter every advance successfully. When the wall was completed in fifty-two days, the enemies lost face and surrounding nations were duly impressed, realizing that God had favored Nehemiah. Thus the prestige of the Jewish state was duly established.

C. Reformation under Ezra, 7—10

Nehemiah next turned his attention to setting up an organized guard system for the entire city. Some parts of Jerusalem were too sparsely settled to have enough people at all points on the wall. Consequently, he called for a registration of all the citizens in the province and recruited some for settlement inside the city.

Before Nehemiah had opportunity to complete his plans, the people gathered in Jerusalem for the religious festivities of the seventh month. Nehemiah gave precedence to the reading of the Law, the observance of the Feast of Trumpets, the Day of Atonement, and the Feast of Tabernacles under the leadership of Ezra the renowned teacher of the Law. After all these festivities and the repeated reading of the Law, the people responded with a pledge to keep the Law as given by Moses. Two laws were singled out for emphasis—intermarriage with the heathen and the keeping of the Sabbath. In a realistic and practical commitment supported by Nehemiah and led by Ezra, the temple ministry was restored.

D. Nehemiah's program and policies, 11—13

Nehemiah now resumed his registration and provided for adequate defense of the city wall by bringing more residents to Jerusalem. The dedication of the walls involved the entire province. Civil and religious leaders and all other participants were organized into two processions. Headed by Ezra and Nehemiah, one proceeded to the right and the other to the left as they marched on the walls of the city. When the two companies met at the temple, a great service of thanksgiving was conducted with music furnished by an orchestra and choirs. With everyone participating, this extensive and joyous celebration and triumphant noise was heard afar.

In 432 B.C., Nehemiah made a trip back to Persia but returned again to Jerusalem. Upon his return, he learned that numerous irregularities had prevailed in allowing strangers into the city and neglecting temple service. Boldly Nehemiah dealt with the offenders, expelling Tobiah the Ammonite and restoring the temple services with a prayer that God might remember his good deeds toward the temple and its staff.

Sabbath observance was next on the reform list. Warning the nobles that this was the sin that had precipitated Judah's captivity and the destruction of Jerusalem, Nehemiah ordered the gates of Jerusalem closed on the Sabbath, even forbidding the arrival of merchants on that day.

Nehemiah also dealt with the problem of mixed marriages. He warned the people that even Solomon had been led into sin through the foreign wives that were brought to Jerusalem. When the grandson of Eliashib the high priest married the daughter of Sanballat the governor of Samaria, he was immediately expelled from Judah by Nehemiah. The account of Nehemiah concludes with the fitting words of his prayer, "Remember me, O my God, for good."

MALACHI'S PROPHECIES The reforms of Nehemiah and Ezra are also reflected in the book of Malachi whose ministry is usually dated during this period (ca. 450-400 B.C.). According to tradition preserved by Josephus, this prophet was the last of God's messengers before the long period of silence, lasting approximately 400 years.

The Messianic expectation is once more projected as the hope for those who fear God. Beginning with the assurance of ultimate victory through the seed of the woman in Genesis 3:15, the Messianic promise had been unfolded in subsequent generations (cf. Gen. 12:3; 49:10; Ex. 3:15; Num. 24:17; II Sam. 7:16; I Chron. 17:14; Isa. 7:14; 9:6, 7; 28:16; Micah 5:2, and others). Malachi points to the terrible day of judgment which will be preceded by mercy in the coming of Elijah (3:1—4:5). In this message of predictive import, the name "Elijah" suggested a time of revival through a God-sent individual who appeared four centuries later as John the Baptist to prepare the way for the Messiah.

In this vivid way, Malachi reminds the godless that they should be afraid of the day of judgment. Those who revere God, however, are assured of God's eternal favor. God's curse rests upon the wicked, while God's blessing is bestowed upon the righteous.

CONCLUDING THE   These three books, which are the main sources
BIBLICAL RECORD   of information about the Jews after the destruc-
OF OLD TESTAMENT   tion of Jerusalem in 586 B.C., conclude the
                        biblical record of Old Testament times, leaving
a long period of silence. Approximately four centuries later the New
Testament opens with the birth of Christ.[3]

Guide Questions for Study and Discussion

1. Who were the leaders of the exiles that returned to Judah?
2. What did they do immediately to establish worship upon arrival in Jerusalem?
3. What two prophets stimulated the Jews to a renewed effort to build the temple?
4. What feast was established as a result of the Jewish deliverance in the days of Esther?
5. What was Ezra's religious interest before returning to Jerusalem?
6. How did Ezra exemplify his concern for divine as well as human aid in helping his people?
7. What was the attitude of Nehemiah toward the plight of his people as reflected in his prayer in chapter one?
8. How did Nehemiah approach the king about his problem?
9. How did Nehemiah organize his efforts to rebuild the walls of Jerusalem?
10. What were the chief reforms by Nehemiah?

Activities for Enrichment and Application

1. Compare the policies toward conquered nations by Assyria, Babylonia, and Persia. Trace the evidences of divine dealings with God's chosen people through these heathen nations.
2. List the qualities of leadership manifested by Nehemiah in facing the opposition by the people of Samaria during this period. What crucial events today test leadership qualities of God's people?
3. Give a summarizing sentence identifying each of the seventeen books in this study.
4. Trace the progressive revelation of the Messianic promises.
5. List what you consider the most important events and their approximate dates covered in this unit of study.

Significant Resources

ADAMSON, J. T. H. "Malachi" in *The New Bible Commentary: Revised.* Ed. by D. Guthrie, J. A. Moyter, A. M. Stibbs, and D. J. Wiseman. Grand Rapids: Wm. B. Eerdmans Pub. Co., 1970.

BENSON, CLARENCE H. *Old Testament Survey: Poetry and Prophecy.* Rev. ed. Wheaton, IL: Evangelical Teacher Training Assn., 1972.

FREE, JOSEPH P. *Archaeology and Bible History.* Wheaton, IL: Scripture Press, 1976.

---

[3] OLD TESTAMENT SURVEY—POETRY AND PROPHECY and NEW TESTAMENT SURVEY provide a profitable sequence study. For a more detailed description, see *Concerning E.T.T.A.,* pp. 95, 96.

Concerning E.T.T.A.

Since 1930 Evangelical Teacher Training Association has been used of God to strengthen and advance evangelical Christian education. E.T.T.A. pioneered in and continues to produce Bible-centered, Christ-honoring leadership preparation materials. These are planned to preserve and propagate the rich Gospel *message* through good educational *methods*.

Christian education is presented as an important factor in the fulfillment of Christ's commission: "Go ye therefore, and teach all nations . . . *teaching* them to observe all things, whatsoever I have commanded you" (Matt. 28:19, 20). In order to minister broadly in the advancement of Christian education, E.T.T.A. functions on three educational levels, each of which complements the others.

THE PRELIMINARY CERTIFICATE PROGRAM

Designed for local church and community leadership preparation classes this program leads to successful teaching for Sunday school teachers and officers. Six vital and challenging subjects are covered — three on Bible Survey and three on Christian Education.

Bible Survey These practical Bible Survey studies are foundational. They show the marvelous unity of the 66 books of the Bible and help one to grasp the central teaching that binds books, chapters, and verses together.

OLD TESTAMENT SURVEY — LAW AND HISTORY

A study of the books of Genesis through Esther giving an overview of God's working among men from creation through the early days of His chosen people.

OLD TESTAMENT SURVEY — POETRY AND PROPHECY

The thrilling messages of the books of Job through Malachi.

NEW TESTAMENT SURVEY

A skillful weaving of the contents of the New Testament books around the central theme — the Person of Christ.

Christian Education These subjects give insight into the pupil's personality problems, ambitions, and needs; give the "know-how" of teaching; present the overall purpose, organization, and program of the Sunday school.

UNDERSTANDING PEOPLE

This study gives insight into pupils' personalities, problems, experiences, interests, and needs.

UNDERSTANDING TEACHING or
TEACHING TECHNIQUES

Alternative texts on teaching methods which show how to communicate biblical truths and apply them to life situations.

SUNDAY SCHOOL SUCCESS

The purpose, organization, and program of the Sunday school.

An award credit card is granted upon completion of each course that is taught by an instructor approved by E.T.T.A. The Preliminary Teachers Certificate is granted when the required 6 courses have been completed. A free booklet of information telling how to start E.T.T.A. classes is available.

THE ADVANCED CERTIFICATE PROGRAM

The Advanced Certificate Program gives a deep understanding of God's Word and an insight into the fields of Christian service. It is offered in E.T.T.A. affiliated Bible institutes* and is profitably presented in local church or community classes. The program consists of a minimum of 12 courses, each 12 lessons in length, and leads to the Advanced Teachers Certificate. It includes the 6 courses of the Preliminary Certificate Program and the following 6 courses.

THE MISSIONARY ENTERPRISE

This study of missions and missionary education gives vision, burden, and "know-how" for challenging new missionary outreach.

EVANGELIZE THRU CHRISTIAN EDUCATION

A challenging consideration of principles and techniques for effective soul winning in the church educational program.

THE TRIUNE GOD

The use of non-technical language makes this spiritually strengthening study of God, Christ, and the Holy Spirit helpful to all.

BIBLICAL BELIEFS

An inspiring study of salvation, inspiration of the Scriptures, the Church, angels, and last things.

CHURCH EDUCATIONAL MINISTRIES or
VACATION BIBLE SCHOOL

These are alternative texts. Church Educational Ministries is a survey of the various educational programs which may be offered in the local church. Vacation Bible School is brimming with proven methods for planning, promoting, and conducting a successful vacation Bible school.

YOUR BIBLE

An enlightening presentation of the origin and authorship of the Bible, how it was preserved, and how we can answer its critics.

THE HIGHER EDUCATION PROGRAM

This specific preparation includes extensive Bible study as well as a wide selection of courses in Christian education and related subjects. It is offered only in institutions of higher education which hold Active membership in E.T.T.A.* A diploma is awarded in recognition of required educational attainment and qualifies the holder to conduct the E.T.T.A. leadership preparation program in church or community classes.

*A list of member schools is available on request.